TRUMPETS

of

BEATEN METAL

Biblical Prayer in Post-biblical Times

by

Eugene A. LaVerdiere, S.S.S.

THE LITURGICAL PRESS
Collegeville, Minnesota

Imprimi potest: Rev. Normand Falardeau, S.S.S., Provincial. *Nihil obstat:* William Heidt, O.S.B., *Censor deputatus.* *Imprimatur:* † George H. Speltz, Bishop of St. Cloud. St. Cloud, Minnesota, July 1, 1974.

To the Students of Blessed Sacrament Seminary

This book is born of a four year experience as director of students at Blessed Sacrament Seminary in Cleveland. Every page is marked by the constructive challenge and support of the seminarians, several of whom are now ordained priests. I dedicate this book to them as an expression of my gratitude.

I also wish to thank in a special way Fathers Francis D. Costa, S.S.S., and Joseph R. Nearon, S.S.S., both of whom were among my professors of theology. They are now my associates on the seminary staff and my colleagues in the Department of Religious Studies at John Carroll University. In many ways I am still their student. Their encouragement, critical evaluation and lively discussion made this book possible.

The countless questions addressed to me by students at John Carroll University, by those who have frequented my public lectures and by the friends with whom I have enjoyed many a pleasant evening of serious discussion have also greatly contributed to this book. I owe special thanks to Doctor Leonard Haas, presently superintendent of Cleveland Psychiatric Institute, and to his wife Mary, to Jack and Dorothy Turcotte, and their families, for providing a friendly fireside forum, for encouraging me to write and for their reading and discussion of the manuscript.

Finally, I am grateful to Judy Bielek for her generous offer of secretarial assistance in preparing the manuscript.

CONTENTS

Introduction

Biblical history is an experiential odyssey of a people's life of prayer. It is the prayer of Hebrews leaving Haran, in search of fulfillment in the way of the Lord. It is the prayer of Israelites turning their backs on the comforts of Egypt and building a temple for the Lord in David's city, of Jews poring over the word of the Lord and penetrating a world united by Alexander. It is the prayer of Christians meeting the same tensions, fears, strivings and joys which filled the life of their biblical forbears as they reached out to the very ends of the earth.

Our efforts at biblical prayer also represent an odyssey, a journey, a search. Contemporary biblical prayer is the life-story of man in search of God, and of God in search of man.

A poor refuge for those who would escape life, the Bible comes to life for those who engage in life. As we learn to recognize ourselves in the struggles, efforts, failures and successes of the great and of the lesser men of biblical history, the Bible's living word is transformed into our personal prayer.

The following chapters represent several years of reflection on that odyssey. Like the Bible, they constitute the record of a search, of a personal search for authenticity in biblical prayer. As readers embark on the same journey, they will recognize themselves, their own questions and their personal reflection in what has been a serious confrontation of the challenge of biblical prayer in post-biblical times. Hopefully, their own search will be facilitated.

Biblical prayer begins with a call, a call to pray with the Scriptures. We must learn to recognize that call in the limited reality of our very own human life. We must become sensitive to the biblical way of praying. Such an awakening sparks a need for study and understanding, not only of the Scriptures, but of ourselves, of life and of our relationship to God, to the universe and to our fellow man.

Biblical prayer springs from the experience of a life truly lived and of a God who is really present. To pray with the Scriptures, we must share in the attitudes reflected in the Scriptures, in a faith founded on God's self-revelation in history and creation, in our history and our own personal universe. We must stir with a charity which reaches out to our fellow man, even to those who wither in their inability to respond. We must look to the future with a hope which is radically open to God's presence.

Let us start in the beginning, when all seems an overwhelming chaos, at that moment of awareness when God says: "Let there be. . . ."

TRUMPETS *of* BEATEN METAL

The Call to Prayer

Lord, teach us to pray.
—Luke 11:1

Is it a dream? Can the life of a merchant patriarch, of a nomadic leader, or of a kingly poet enlighten us? Can the word of biblical historians, uncompromising prophets and eastern sages really speak to us? Can the Psalms actually voice our personal prayer? Two millennia, and far more than two millennia, separate us from the good news of Jesus and the flame of Pentecost. We live in the heady and at times overwhelming climate of an emerging nuclear and computerized civilization, whose home is megalopolis and whose frontier is planetary space. Could we be further away from the warmth and intimacy of weekly gatherings in an upper room?

High on the *tell* of western history, countless strata separate us from the Sion and Calvary bedrock deep below. We stand above the charred debris of world conflicts and revolutions. Below us, the splendid humanism of the Renaissance and the theological intellectualism of the Middle Ages. Paris, Bologna, Oxford and Cambridge lie flat upon centuries of feudal life and Islamic threat. The legal and organizational columns of Rome protrude dizzily upwards through the ruins of Byzantium, their sturdy base buried in obscurity. From the shattered vessel of modern Christianity, the narrow trench to our Christian origins must sort its way through the many layers of reform, renewal, struggle and division before opening onto the peaceful hills and plains of Galilee. Here we stand, high on the *tell* of science, language, architecture and the arts. How can we seriously hope to reach Bethlehem, Nazareth, Capernaum, Jerusalem, the Sinai and Haran?

There was a time when

> The Sons of Aaron would sound a blast,
> the priests, on their trumpets of beaten metal;
> A blast to resound mightily
> as a reminder before the Most High.
>
> Then all the people with one accord
> would quickly fall prostrate to the ground
> In adoration before the Most High,
> before the Holy One of Israel.
>
> Then hymns would re-echo,
> and over the throng sweet strains of praise resound.
> All the people of the land would shout for joy,
> praying to the Merciful One (Sirach 50:16-18).

Israel's trumpet call to prayer! Is that blast no more than a dying echo? Surely, it still resounds. But where are the throngs, the sweet strains of praise and the joyful shouts?

The Bible sits open before us. We read, we listen carefully and do not understand. We look intently but perceive nothing. Nothing bores like the word of God. Isaiah's prophetic commission had been "to make the heart of this people sluggish, to dull their ears and close their eyes" (Is. 6:10). Will God not speak to us? Isaiah's victims, we turn the pages. Verse upon verse, entire chapters, pass before our eyes, cold and detached.

Through Jeremiah, the Lord had promised that he would place his law within us and write it upon our hearts (Jer. 31:33). Has Jeremiah deceived us? True, God is not dead. But the Bible?

Perhaps we need only be more attentive. What is the biblical writer saying? What does he mean by that word, phrase, unit? We study.

> We pick among dead bones beneath fluorescent
> light,
> bore into the grammar of the truth.
>
> —*John L'Heureux*[1]

Grammar. Philology. Literary analysis. Is there nothing more? Surely God must be a poet, but where is the poetry? Where has the spirit gone? That Spirit through which we once cried "Abba!" (Rom. 8:15)? Was Paul deluded?

> Nothing bores like the word of God
> made grammar: blunted reeds rammed
> into our ears — not shaken by the wind
> but rattled in an angry hand that knows
> no gentle touch. No soft animal warms
> beneath it, no seed grows to promise.
>
> —*John L'Heureux*[1]

In our deepest self, we stand in awe before our biblical forbears at prayer. We marvel at the facility with which their most personal sentiments found expression in ancient biblical forms. From the prayer of an inspired poet, the Psalms had become the prayer of many faithful generations. They became the prayer of Peter, James and John. The biblical

[1] John L'Heureux, "God, Dying," in *One Eye and a Measuring Rod.* New York, The Macmillan Company, 1968, p. 78.

word, with its songs and stories, countless laws and unending lists struck in them a vital response. The word spoke to them, and with it they spoke to God.

Is it awe, or rather envy that we experience as our efforts lead into a vast desert separating us from the ancient Israelite and early Christian at prayer? Are we then sons of Cain, banished from a primeval oasis once intended for our living space? A people condemned by culture, technology and a dulling span of years to roam in a land east of Eden where there is no living water nor life-giving bread?

We turn the pages of Scripture with historical nostalgia, recalling the days when it was not so, when heroic Christians like Jerome, Augustine, Francis and Dominic found a ready expression for their deepest feelings in the sacred text. Could an ancient psalm really have been their personal prayer?

Envy breeds guilt as we observe some of our own contemporaries, for whom the Scriptures appear so personally meaningful. Therese de Lisieux? A cloistered child. Surely a foreigner. Charles de Foucauld? A restless soul in a biblical wilderness, a tiny living cell on the earth's wasting scab. Hardly a contemporary. But Dietrich Bonhoeffer? Enlightened, experienced, clearly one of us:

> God's speech in Jesus Christ meets us in the Holy Scriptures. If we wish to pray with confidence and gladness, then the words of Holy Scripture will have to be the solid basis of our prayer. For here we know that Jesus Christ, the Word of God, teaches us to pray. The words which come from God become, then, the steps on which we find our way to God.[2]

[2] Dietrich Bonhoeffer, *Psalms: the Prayer Book of the Bible.* Minneapolis, Augsburg Publishing House, 1970, pp. 11-12.

Is it that we have made no effort to take those steps? Is it that we have wandered into another way?

> Our dear Lord, who has given to us and taught us to pray the Psalter and the Lord's Prayer, grants to us also the spirit of prayer and of grace so that we pray with enthusiasm and earnest faith, properly and without ceasing, for we need to do this; he has asked for it and therefore wants to have it from us. To him be praise, honor, and thanksgiving. Amen. (Martin Luther).[3]

Jesus was a good teacher. He may have had poor students.

Even more disturbing is the elderly gentleman in each one's experience, silent simplicity with Bible in hand, pages aging, yellowed, worn not with time, but with use. His placid features are those of Moses descending from God's holy mountain. Israelites, every one of us, we turn away, blinded by the reflection of God's glory. We stand at a distance, unworthy. Have we been locked out of a secret by some trick of birth or circumstance? Our journey to Jerusalem seems so long, his so short. We travel in the company of love, like men unable to love. Unbelievers in a worshipping community, we walk, lonely and alone. Yes,

> We are the hollow men
> We are the stuffed men
> Leaning together
> Headpiece filled with straw. Alas!
> Our dried voices, when
> We whisper together
> Are quiet and meaningless
> As wind in dry grass
> Or rats' feet over broken glass
> In our dry cellar

[3] As quoted by D. Bonhoeffer, *ibid.*, p. 63.

> Shape without form, shade without colour,
> Paralysed force, gesture without motion.
>
> — *T. S. Eliot*[4]

Where is the living God of Abraham, Isaac and Jacob?

The Scriptures have become a stony tomb, sealed against our entry. Ages of religious experience, God's very word, lie buried therein, usually in deathly silence, at most in muted, undecipherable sound. Like the Galilean women at dawn on the third day we ask: Who will roll away the stone for us? Who will transform that sound into a living word?

Is it the voice of the prophet which has grown weak? Or is it our hearing which has grown dull? Can it be that à Kempis has a message for us?

> Whoever wishes to understand and fully savor the words of Christ must seek to conform his life to that of Christ.[5]

O God, that we may hear! "Lord, teach us to pray" (Luke 11:1).

> The disciples want to pray, but they do not know how to do it. That can be very painful, to want to speak with God and not to be able to, to have to be speechless before God, to discover that every call to him dies within itself, that heart and mouth speak an absurd language which God does not want to hear. —*Dietrich Bonhoeffer*[6]

We are the disciples. We have tasted that dying word. "Lord, teach us to pray." But how could we have been so blind. Our very petition is biblical

[4] T. S. Eliot, *The Complete Poems and Plays.* New York, Harcourt, Brace & Company, 1952, p. 56.

[5] Book 1, chapter 1, par. 2.

[6] Dietrich Bonhoeffer, *op. cit.,* p. 10.

prayer. Already the stone has been rolled away. The sound has become a word! Like the deportees in Babylon, we had cried: "How could we sing a song of the Lord in a foreign land?" (Ps. 137:4). With Isaiah we had exclaimed: "I am a man of unclean lips" (Is. 6:5). With Jeremiah: "Ah, Lord God! I know not how to speak; I am too young" (Jer. 1:6). Fallen upon our face with Ezekiel, a voice speaks loud and clear: "Son of man, stand up! I wish to speak with you" (2:1). Ours now to eat the scroll (Ez. 2:1-3). No longer are we strangers, unloving and alone.

It was a dream, but not a meaningless dream. Like unrecognizing disciples already in the presence of Christ, we merely failed to recognize the biblical quality of our personal prayer.

Our expectations led us astray. Realistic expectations sensitize the eye to discovery. Misdirected expectations frustrate recognition. We expected a plant in full flower and failed to recognize the seedling. Placing the young plant aside, we went about seeking the living among the dead.

Our expectations were simplistic, unreal, divorced from the life and death situations which underlie the biblical word. Apart from a searching, fearing and trusting spirit's experience of God, the Scriptures are meaningless. We expected it would be easy. We thought we could pray with the Scriptures comfortably, without leaving Haran or setting out into the desert. We never seriously considered the ascent of Calvary. We thought being purified like fire-tried gold was a matter of words, a lovely figure of speech.

We were wrong. Biblical prayer is firmly grounded in historical faith. Uprooted from its faith-setting, it quickly dies, leaving a soulless corpse. Faithless, lifeless, man utters his prayer to stone images of his own raising.

Why had we not brought our problem to the Scriptures? Biblical faith itself was constantly challenged by a present and future which seemed out of step with religious and historical expectations. One example would have sufficed. In the sixth century B.C., with the temple destroyed, the Holy City in ruins and themselves in exile, the Israelites had little courage to sing the ancient songs of Sion. "How can we sing a song of the Lord in a foreign land?" But out of their inability to pray, they prayed. They groped. Blindly, they searched. Stripped of all but their relationship with God, they slowly opened their eyes in new understanding. The God of their fathers was here in their midst, here in far-off Babylon. "Give thanks to the God of heaven, for his mercy endures forever" (Ps. 136:26).

As so often before, the Israelites faced and accepted the challenge of historical faith. How could they have doubted the presence of their God? Israel's new understanding rested on a reinterpretation of the past. A deeply troubled people refocused its expectations in recognition of present reality. With faith renewed, prayer no longer appeared disincarnate and meaningless. Biblical prayer was truly their prayer, just as surely as the Lord was their God, and they his people.

The Scriptures voice the mature faith of understanding individuals. The high quality and simplicity of their literary work represents not the spontaneous simplicity of the child but the conscious, self-possessed and acquired simplicity of an adult. Very few in the biblical period rose to this level of religious experience and understanding. Still fewer had the gift to express their faith as we find it recorded in the Scriptures.

Biblical prayer reflects the growth and development of each individual person no less than the history of the entire community of God's people. No true son of Abraham was born fully mature. The prayer of David's warrior years was hardly that of the accomplished royal poet. When we turn to Peter, the apostolic leader, humbly deferring admission of his love for Christ, we should recall the frightened disciple who could not so much as acknowledge his acquaintance with Jesus.

Yes, it was a dream, but a meaningful dream. Its interpretation lay there all along before our unseeing eyes. Like our biblical forbears, we needed only to adjust our expectations for its meaning to be plain.

What right had we to expect that somehow we might pray with the Scriptures while rejecting the challenge of historical faith? Peter, Paul, and even Jesus, they too stood on a *tell.* Biblical prayer cannot be a return to the past. It is an acceptance of the present.

What right had we to think ourselves the spiritual and personal equals of biblical history's soaring spirits? All were not Paul. The assembly listened as the apostle spoke, grateful to share in his gift.

What right had we to presume ourselves at ease with the prayer of those who had arrived at the personal maturity of a highly integrated faith? We stand at the very threshold of faith experience, beginners, slowly making our way to Christian adulthood.

Could we be further away from the warmth and intimacy of weekly gatherings in an upper room? The distance from the foot of the Cross and the circus of Nero may have been greater.

Biblical Prayer

According to the Scriptures.
—1 Cor. 15:4

Only "the fool says in his heart, 'There is no God' " (Ps. 14:1; 53:2). Only the fool refuses to pray. Since prayer is man's normal response to a personal God, the Scriptures find no need to urge us to pray. They instruct us rather on how to pray.

> This is how you are to pray:
> Our Father in heaven,
> hallowed be your name,
> your kingdom come,
> your will be done
> on earth as it is in heaven.
> Give us today our daily bread,
> and forgive us the wrong we have done
> as we forgive those who wrong us.
> Subject us not to trial
> but deliver us from the evil one.
> If you forgive the faults of others, your heavenly Father will forgive you yours. If you do not forgive others, neither will your Father forgive you (Matthew 6:9-15).

They present the attitudes required for prayer.

> When you are praying, do not behave like the hypocrites who love to stand and pray in synagogues or on street corners in order to be noticed. I give you my word, they are already repaid. When-

> ever you pray, go to your room, close the door, and pray to your Father in private. Then your Father, who sees what no man sees, will repay you. In your prayer do not rattle on like the pagans. They think they will win a hearing by the sheer multiplication of words. Do not imitate them. Your Father knows what you need before you ask him (Matthew 6:5-8).

They urge constancy in prayer.

> Never cease praying, render constant thanks; such is God's will for you in Christ Jesus (I Thess. 5:17-18).

They even indicate some of the intentions for which we must pray, for example,

> I urge that petitions, prayers, intercessions, and thanksgivings be offered for all men, especially for kings and those in authority, that we may be able to lead undisturbed and tranquil lives in perfect piety and dignity (I Tim. 2:1-2).

Above all, however, the Scriptures teach us that we must pray "according to the Scriptures."

In turning to the Scriptures for prayer, we stand in the truest line of Old Testament tradition. The Bible was created by people who could not forget their history. When they prayed, they did so in the memory of the heroes of their faith and of the mighty things God had wrought for them. At first, they prayed with their unwritten heritage, with their traditional songs and stories, handed down over many generations. As the Bible gradually took form, increasingly they prayed with the Scriptures, with the Law, the Prophets and the Writings.

The New Testament, which gradually emerged from the life and worship of the Christian community, stands as a clear witness to the biblical roots of early Christian prayer. The Our Father, for example, which was the Christian community's characteristic prayer, voiced the specific identity of the followers of Jesus. This prayer, which to this day unites all Christians as sons of one Father, is incomprehensible apart from the first century interpretation of biblical tradition. The mode of prayerful expression which is found in the "thanksgiving" sections of Paul's letters also reflects the vitality of biblical prayer. All of early Christian prayer, personal as well as communal, was profoundly biblical, both in its use of ancient formulae, such as the Psalms, and in its adaptation of biblical tradition.

Old and New Testament cultus provided a sphere of life in which biblical tradition and literature were maintained as a living force. In temple, home and synagogue, the ancient Hebrew, Israelite, Jew and Christian quickened the memory of divine communication. In worshipping faith, the mute symbols sprang to life. In communal and personal prayer, the record of God's word took flesh and spirit.

Many biblical works were actually written to meet the needs of worship. Historical faith was formulated in view of the various celebrations which marked the yearly cycle at Israel's ancient shrines. The early work of the Deuteronomist must be viewed in relation to worship at the northern sanctuary of Shechem. Most of the Psalms were born of cultic need at Jerusalem's great temple. Many works which originally had been intended for Canaanite sanctuaries or for the many Israelite shrines were re-edited to serve in Jerusalem's temple worship.

After the destruction of the temple in Jerusalem (587 B.C.) and the deportation of Israel's spiritual, intellectual and political leaders to Babylon, biblical tradition and literature were associated with more humble contexts. The home became a place of worship. Community gathering places became houses of prayer. As of the third century before Christ, synagogues sprang up in all the lands of the Diaspora, in Israel, and even in Jerusalem, wherever there were Israelites to worship.

A worshipping people needed to pray in its own language. In the Nile delta, where synagogues dotted the towns, villages and the hellenistic capital of Alexandria, the Old Testament was translated into Greek. In Babylon and Palestine, it was rendered into the vernacular Aramaic.

In Jesus' day, the Scriptures provided a source of historical self-understanding, a stimulus to prophetic awakening and the elements of practical wisdom. The devout Jew studied, interpreted and discussed the Scriptures. So it was with Jesus, whom the New Testament presents as prophet, sage and interpreter of religious history.

Study was oriented to worship. Reflection on the Scriptures readied the ground for prayer. The very place of study was built adjoining the synagogue. In searching the Scriptures, Jesus and his contemporaries found a divinely-inspired formulation of prayer for nearly every conceivable attitude and experiential situation.

The priestly tradition had long viewed every living moment as an expression of worship. In the sixth and fifth centuries B.C., its theology of life had given the Torah its definitive stamp. In the first century, the Pharisees stood in the same tradition. Worship flowed out of the temple and the numerous synagogues into the homes and streets of the city.

At daybreak, a devout Jew such as Jesus recited the *Shema,* "Hear, O Israel, the Lord our God is the only God" (Deut. 6:4). He recalled the divine commandment to love God with his whole self (Deut. 6:5). To his profession of faith and moral commitment he added the words of Deut. 5:6-9; 11:13-21 and Num. 15:41. After the *Shema,* he prayed the *Tephillah,* a collection of biblically inspired blessings known as the Great Blessing.

> Blessed be thou, Lord our God and the God
> of our fathers,
> the God of Abraham, the God of Isaac and the
> God of Jacob,
> God great, mighty and fearful,
> most high God,
> master of heaven and earth,
> our shield and the shield of our fathers,
> our trust in every generation.
> Blessed be thou, Lord, the shield of Abraham.

During Jesus' life, these blessings were relatively few. By the end of the century, the original nucleus had developed into the eighteen — now nineteen — blessings well-known to our Jewish contemporaries.

Around 3 P.M., during the afternoon sacrifice, a trumpet sounded over the roof-tops of Jerusalem. In the markets, at the wells and public cisterns, in the tightly woven web of streets and alleyways, in the privacy of the homes and in all the public places, business and other activities paused for a moment of prayer. Devout Jews everywhere united themselves once again in praying the *Tephillah* with those who had assembled in the courts of the temple for the sacrifice. The call to prayer was part of life's daily expectations. With the fading sound of the trumpet, life resumed its tempo. Shalom. Peace.

With the sun's setting, day ended as it had begun. In the tradition of his fathers, each Jew recited the *Shema,* recalling his obligation to teach it to his children (Deut. 6:6-7). He prayed the *Tephillah.* Thus it was, that for Jesus and his followers, along with their fellow Jews, biblical prayer marked the hours of daily existence.

The early Christians continued in the Jewish traditions of their formative years. They attended synagogue regularly, as had been Jesus' custom. Like him, they frequented the temple. In the course of their meals with Jesus, they had come to know and love him. In his presence, they had found true nourishment. After his passion and death, they gathered together for "the breaking of the bread," their distinctive fellowship meal, now known as the Eucharist.

The Christians assembled on the morrow of the Sabbath, on the day of the Lord, when they celebrated Jesus' risen life. Rejoicing in the good news of Jesus' Lordship, they recalled his prophetic teaching, powerful in word and deed. So little had they understood! Imbued with Christ's Spirit, they grew in their knowledge of the Risen Lord. The words and deeds of Jesus acquired new and undreamed-of significance. Jesus' life, death and resurrection had truly been "according to the Scriptures."

The assembled community listened intently to the teaching of the apostles. They expressed mutual fellowship and common life in Christ. They shared in the breaking of the bread and in the customary prayers (Acts 2:42). As little by little they moved away from the synagogue, they adapted the traditional synagogue service as an introduction to their eucharistic meal.

From one point of view, the Bible is a classical account of actual prayer. The cultic context of ancient Israel and early Christianity is reflected in both its style and content.

The first seven chapters of the book of Leviticus are entirely concerned with the ritual to be followed in Israelite holocausts, cereal offerings, communion or peace offerings and expiatory sacrifices. The book of Deuteronomy includes ancient Israel's profession of historical faith. "My father was a wandering Aramean" (26:5-9). So prayed every Israelite as he offered the first-fruits of his labor in thanksgiving for the harvest.

In his first letter to the Christians at Corinth, Paul assembled the traditional elements of the Christian community's response to the preaching of the apostles. 1 Cor. 15:3-5 is an expression of faith in the meaning of Jesus' death and resurrection:

> Christ died for our sins in accordance with the Scriptures; he was buried; he rose on the third day in accordance with the Scriptures; he was seen by Cephas.

The entire Christian world stood united in its profession of this earliest of creeds.

Liturgical hymns and formulae abound in the New Testament. The baptismal hymn in 1 Peter (1:3-5), the christological hymn in Paul's letter to the Christians at Philippi (2:6-11) and the paean to the eternal word made flesh in the prologue of John's Gospel (1:1-18) provide excellent examples. By praying the Our Father in a eucharistic context, today's Christians stand in a tradition which originated in the Christian community's formative years. The Our Father was inscribed in the Gospels of Matthew (6:9-13) and Luke (11:2-4) as well as in that early second-century work we know as the *Didache.* No Christian is unfamiliar with the words of eucharistic interpretation quoted in the traditional accounts of Jesus' last supper. The greetings and blessings found in the opening and closing verses of Paul's letters were surely influenced by the liturgy. "Grace and peace from God our Father and the Lord Jesus Christ" (Rom. 1:7). "To him, the God who alone is wise, may glory be given through Jesus Christ unto endless ages. Amen" (Rom. 16:27).

The entire Bible is a prayer, a prayer which began with Abraham four thousand years ago and ended with the last verses of 2 Peter early in the second century A.D. When Abraham's voice weakened, another voice took up his prayer and spoke it loud and strong. So it was for two thousand years, with voice succeeding voice and prayer rising above prayer, each one taking up the word of the past and giving it new life. Nations and empires rose and fell, but always there was one to gather up the dying fragments into a new and living synthesis.

How sad that that prayer should have ended. But did it end? The Bible has always been considered especially suited for the prayer and meditative reading of Jews and Christians. What of the great Rabbis and the Fathers of the Church? Did they not continue the prayer which Abraham began? What of the living Church and Synagogue? The Bible is a prayer which never did end. Of its very nature, it is an unfinished prayer.

For us to pray with the Scriptures, we have only to share in the experience and attitudes which underlie the biblical word. Are we really men of worship like the Israelites and early Christians whose prayer we would speak? How can we become biblical men of prayer? These are the questions we must ask. Only the fool refuses to pray with the Scriptures.

Discovering the Scriptures

Though they contain some obscure passages.
—2 Peter 3:16

We have heard the call to prayer, a call to pray "according to the Scriptures." We have heard its trumpet sound in the rush of our cities and the quiet of our countryside, in the streets and houses of everyman's Jerusalem. "Lord, teach us to pray." Refocusing our expectations, we have isolated some of our difficulties at praying with the Scriptures and found them to be normal difficulties. In ancient times, those same difficulties provided the spark needed for the formation of biblical literature.

Difficulties? Challenges is a more accurate term, intellectual, experiential and attitudinal challenges. How little we know of our biblical heritage, of those two thousand years of religious tradition and literature which have shaped our history. How limited our experience, how circumscribed our attitudes in comparison with the great men and women whose prayer-life we would share.

The most obvious challenge is intellectual. For many years, the volume and quality of scientific studies on the Bible have indicated its roots in ancient life and culture. What did a biblical work mean for its writer? What did Paul actually say to the Christians of Corinth in the 50's of our era? How was his letter interpreted by its intended readers, by the community assembled at the house of Stephanas? There is no evading these questions.

And so we must study. We must examine the challenge, explicate it, circumscribe it. We must reflect on ourselves as we try to cope with its tension, the polarity of biblical and personal prayer. We must seek out a good approach to the challenge, a biblical approach. We must focus on our response, on the tools we shall use, interpretation, exegesis. We must test our approach and response against that of the Bible itself. Mark, the earliest evangelist, will provide the criterion. The challenge, the tension, the approach, the response, the test—five simple lessons to intellectual freedom.

The Challenge

Biblical literature springs from a way of life and a tradition of writing. It expresses a people's reflection on experience. Its forms, phrases and words are heavily weighted with an entire history of associations which can hardly be divorced from their meaning. Its literary techniques are unusual to us.

There is the inclusion, whereby a literary unit is framed within a set of key words or expressions. In the Emmaus account, we are told that Jesus approached the disciples and walked along with them. "However, they were restrained from *recognizing him*" (Luke 24:16). A problem has been set forth, the inability to recognize the risen Lord. A strong undercurrent of expectation permeates the entire narrative. The tension is resolved in the breaking of the bread. "With that their eyes were opened and they *recognized him*" (Luke 24:31).

There are also various types of parallelism, characteristic of the oral forms which lie so close beneath the surface of biblical literature. In a synonymous parallelism the second member develops a metaphor or repeats the idea of the first, but with a slight variation.

> The door turns on its hinges,
> the sluggard, on his bed! (Proverbs 26:14).

A parallelism is antithetic when the second member contrasts with the first.

> He who winks at a fault causes trouble,
> but he who frankly reproves promotes peace
> (Proverbs 10:10).

A sensitive examination of the Scriptures reveals many variations in parallel structure. A favorite device was the synonymous and antithetic chiasm, in which the terms of the second member are inverted.

> Have mercy on me, O God, in your goodness;
> in the greatness of your compassion wipe out my offense (Ps. 51:3).
> A fountain of life is the mouth of the just,
> but the mouth of the wicked conceals violence
> (Proverbs 10:11).

Nearly every sentence or paragraph challenges our understanding. There are technical terms such as "wisdom," the "word," "regeneration," and the "law," all of which possess a cosmic, an historical and an experiential dimension. These terms have meaning in twentieth-century vocabulary, but the biblical writers used them differently. There are unusual expressions such as "to die with Christ," and "to rise with Christ," expressions meant to shed light on Christian baptism but which we relate to our own experience with great difficulty.

We do not recognize the geographical designations, the measures, the currency, the administrative functions, the religious roles and the social attitudes. What was it like to live in first-century Capernaum? How far is sixty stadia? What is a talent or a mite? Why are tax collectors classed with sinners? What is the position of a procurator? How can a shepherd be called the door of the sheep? Whence the tension between Jews and Samaritans, the conflicts between Pharisees and Sadducees and the negative Judean image of Galileans? So many questions, so many mysteries.

The challenge is clear. We are confronted with a literary and historical situation which is foreign to us. How can the prayer of another people, living in another time and place be our personal prayer? How can we pray both biblically and spontaneously?

The Tension

Both biblical and spontaneous or personal prayer are deeply inscribed in Israelite tradition. In ancient times, biblical prayer was in fact personal prayer, the personal prayer of the one who created or recorded it and of the communities for which it was intended. In our own times, the double focus of interest on these two forms of prayer witnesses to the vitality of Christian tradition. The gospel word of God, planted at the moment of Christianity's conception truly abides forever. After these many centuries, it still lives incorruptible in the spirit of Christianity.

Our focus on both biblical and spontaneous prayer, however, is not without inner tension. The one constantly threatens the other. Far from a new phenomenon in Christian experience, this very tension provided the stimulus for the development of biblical literature itself. As ancient works no longer expressed current religious attitudes, new works were created. Fresh shoots sprang up from Israel's ancient stock to recapitulate the past in relation to actual experience.

The tension between biblical and spontaneous prayer is not an isolated phenomenon but a specific manifestation of basic tensions inherent in Christian existence. It is a normal tension for anyone who would commit himself personally to an historical and social religion. The Christian actually and personally lives his religion in history and community.

Every effort to remove the tension between biblical and spontaneous prayer attacks the very nature of biblical prayer, which was both "according to the Scriptures" or traditions accepted at the time, and spontaneous. It was authentically personal as well as in the Spirit. The tension encountered can be eliminated only at the cost of biblical prayer itself. The challenge of biblical prayer is to maintain the tension by keeping its poles in balance.

Our tendency to escape the tension is strong. We can destroy it, first by denying ourselves the spontaneity of prayer. Let us pray. Let us pray with words provided by the Scriptures. "Our Father in heaven . . . look upon . . . do not . . . Amen!" Somewhere in those solemn intonations we have lost the very self who yearned to pray. The personal element has all but disappeared. Formal prayer. Such prayer has value, does it not? It is the prayer of the Church. Surely it is pleasing to God and efficacious.

Is this praying with the Scriptures? We have not prayed the Bible, we have quoted it. Is this prayer? Or has prayer itself vanished with the personal element? In a Christian community which is avid for authentic personal prayer, impersonal "biblical prayer" is frequently abandoned altogether. True prayer is undertaken independently of the Scriptures.

The tension may also be destroyed by eliminating the biblical pole. We continue to pray with the Scriptures but in so highly subjective a manner that the biblical quality of our prayer is questionable. Prayer is cast in a biblical mold, but the biblical text has little relationship to the meaning attributed to it. We speak of prayer in the Spirit. Such prayer must have value! Surely prayer in the Spirit is pleasing to God!

Once again, we have quoted the Bible without really praying it. We have all but materially detached our personal prayer from its biblical roots. Prayer there may be, but speaking to God with emptied shells of biblical words cannot be called biblical prayer.

The Approach

Since the tension in biblical prayer is a biblical phenomenon, we might do well to turn to the Scriptures in our efforts to maintain the needed balance. The Bible is normative for Christian life and attitudes in many ways. Its message is normative. Its creative tension between traditional and personal prayer is also normative. Why should the biblical approach to this tension not be equally normative?

The attitudes of biblical man were not fatalistic. He did not merely accept a difficulty. He responded to it. For centuries, response came in the way of expanding and re-editing ancient works. A biblical book thus represented an organic process. It had a history. This is true of the Pentateuch, for example, and of the work of certain prophets like First-Isaiah (Is. 1—39) and Ezekiel. A work could also be brought up to date by adding a new section to it. At different periods of history, Second-Isaiah (Is. 40—55) and Third-Isaiah (Is. 56—65) were thus joined to First-Isaiah. Mark 16:9-20 was appended to the earliest extant written Gospel. Finally, the response could consist in an entirely new work, such as that of the Chronicler (1, 2 Chronicles, Ezra, Nehemiah) or the various works which make up the New Testament. The normalcy of these procedures is evidenced by those Christians who ask why the Bible could not be expanded to include modern works or rewritten to meet contemporary needs or even why an entirely new Bible could not be written for our times.

Even with the writing of new works, however, older biblical literature did not cease to exercise an influence. On the contrary, when the New Testament was in formation, much of the Old Testament had become canonized and normative, for Jewish and Christian life.

In the fifth century B.C., following Israel's return from Babylon, the Torah was viewed with such respect that no one would have thought of adding or subtracting from it. The Book of Moses had become sacred literature, the written record of God's word. Within a relatively short time, the Israelites found themselves in a situation very similar to ours. The distance grew ever greater between the life-conditions which gave birth to the Torah and the rapidly changing milieu of Israelite life. The Torah became less and less applicable. No longer did it reflect the experience of Israel. The mirror of life had lost its lustre. Who could understand it?

Israel's approach to this situation was the *Beth-Sepher,* a kind of elementary Bible School, and the *Beth-Hamidrash,* a secondary Bible School. If the Scriptures were to be maintained as a living force in Israel's life and prayer, they had to be studied.

So it was in biblical times, and so it is today. Good editions of the Bible, with explanatory notes and introductions, this is our *Beth-Sepher.* Books, articles, commentaries on the Scriptures, lectures and discussions with scholars, this is our *Beth-Hamidrash.*

The Response

For centuries, the technical term to designate the study of the Scriptures has been exegesis. The word was originally a Greek noun meaning, first of all, a description or a narrative. So it appears in Greek classical literature, in Hellenistic literature as well as in biblical literature. We find it for example in one of the most important Greek manuscripts of the book of Judges, the *Codex Vaticanus,* where Gideon is said to have heard the description *(exegesis)* and explanation *(synkrisis)* of a dream (7:15). Of its very nature, such a narrative or exegesis implied a degree of interpretation.

Sensitive to the interpretational dimension of the narrative art, ancient authors also used the word directly in the sense of explanation and interpretation. Telling the story of Esther, Josephus refers to "the Seven Persians, who have charge of the interpretation *(exegesis)* of the laws among them" (Antiquities, XI, 192). Laws obviously needed to be interpreted in the light of new and changing situations.

When the Scriptures, no longer appeared relevant or applicable to Jewish life, they too needed to be interpreted. For Philo, a first-century Jewish philosopher, "The exposition *(exegesis)* of the sacred scriptures treats the inner meaning conveyed in allegory" *(De Vita Contemplativa,* 78). In his view, the words have become a symbolic covering, an outward and visible sign, in which the exegete must discern the inward and hidden meaning.

Every narrative presentation of an event is an interpretation. In narrating the story of Jesus, for example, the Gospel writers interpreted the traditions handed down in the Christian communities. They interpreted them in relation to their intended readers, adapting their material to Christians of Greek origin or of Jewish origin, to mixed communities, as well as to the historical experience of their readers. The Christians of the 80's for whom Matthew and Luke wrote could not be approached in the same manner as those of the 60's who constituted Mark's intended readership. They also interpreted tradition within the context of Israelite and Jewish history and literature, in the light of their own experience, of their theological insights and of their specific literary intentions. The evangelists were truly exegetes, that is, narrators and interpreters of Christian tradition.

In its effort to shed light on the ancient text, exegesis has become increasingly diversified. In our own time, it has become a highly technical study invoking various methods and techniques developed in relation to the many aspects of biblical literature.

It studies the meaning of ancient words and expressions, investigates the styles of the various authors, and the literary forms they utilized. It explores the relationships among various biblical writings, tries to unveil the oral traditions which underlie the present written work and even probes into the nature of the historical events which provided the point of departure for biblical literature. Such exegesis is not an end in itself, but an effort to provide a scientific set of notes, an aid to greater understanding. It is meant to facilitate our reading and praying of the Scriptures.

The Test

When Mark set about writing his narrative of the Christian event, oral traditions had become fairly stereotyped. Mark chose not to ignore these traditional formulations, even though in many cases their setting in life had become quite foreign to his readers.

By force of historical circumstance and by the nature of his task, Mark became an interpreter in two senses. He interpreted Christian traditions first by structuring their presentation in view of his theological, literary and pastoral intentions. This is clearly the most fundamental function of interpretation, which aims at making a piece of tradition or a work of literature meaningful to a new audience. Today, the word hermeneutics is reserved for this first and most important function of interpretation.

Second, Mark interpreted the Christian traditions by interrupting the course of his narrative with various editorial comments. To grasp the relevance of a passage, the reader needed to understand the original context and meaning of a word or expression. Today, such informational material would be termed exegesis.

The relationship between these two functions of interpretation is already clear from the work of Mark. Exegesis, the informational material which Mark supplies, is meant to serve and facilitate his hermeneutic of Christian tradition.

Mark's exegetical comments were of various kinds. He could not presume that his readers would understand various Aramaic expressions included in the traditional accounts. These he translated. The story of the resurrection of Jairus' daughter stated that Jesus took her by the hand and said "*Talitha, koum*, which means," says Mark, "Little girl, get up" (5:41). In like manner, he points out that *korban* means "dedicated to God" (7:11), *Ephphatha* is translated "Be opened" (7:34), *Abba* is the equivalent of "O Father" (14:36), *Golgotha* of "Skull Place" (15:22), and *Eloi, Eloi, lama sabachthani* of "My God, my God, why have you forsaken me?" (15:34).

At times Mark found he needed to explain the nature of a custom: "They had observed a few of his disciples eating meals without having purified—that is to say, washed—their hands" (7:2); or even to provide historical information and Jewish background to clarify incidents in the life of Jesus: "The Pharisees, and in fact all Jews, cling to the customs of their ancestors, and never eat without scrupulously washing their hands. Moreover, they never eat anything from the market without first sprinkling it. There are many other traditions they observe—for example, the washing of cups and jugs and kettles" (7:3-4).

Mark's Gospel includes several other interpretational aids. It indicates for example that the Sadducees hold there is no resurrection (12:18), that the hall into which the soldiers led Jesus during the Passion was known as the praetorium (15:16) and that Preparation Day refers to the eve of the Sabbath (15:42). On occasion he found it necessary to identify a personage: "Joseph from Arimathea arrived—a distinguished member of the Sanhedrin" (15:42); "a man Simon of Cyrene, the father of Alexander and Rufus, was coming from the fields" (15:21).

Like the traditions which Mark himself had used, his literary account of the Gospel came increasingly in need of interpretation. The story had to be re-told, re-interpreted. We owe two further Gospel accounts, that according to Matthew and that according to Luke, to this awareness of Mark's inadequacy. Both of these Gospels utilized the traditional Marcan account, but they re-wrote it entirely. At times they quoted from it directly, but they supplemented it with further traditional material. In view of their own interpretation of the Christ-event, they also altered its vocabulary and its ordering of events. In so doing, they added a great deal of information concerning Jesus' times and Jewish culture.

Although for a time Mark's work was partially eclipsed in the life of the Christian community, it was not entirely displaced. The fact that Matthew and Luke relied on it so heavily indicates to what extent it already commanded the respect of Christians. In an effort to adapt it to the gospel needs of the community, several new endings were appended to it. By the end of the second century, however, Mark's Gospel had become untouchable. Along with the other accounts of the Gospel, it stood with the

Old Testament as an integral part of the Christian Scriptures.

The canonization of Mark's Gospel marks the beginning of its modern exegesis. Interpretative aids had to be developed. These were not included as editorial comments in the Marcan text, but added to it by way of exegetical commentary.

Mark's editorial comments had supplied various kinds of information. With the passage of time, the type of information needed would become even more varied. Readers would no longer be familiar with some of his literary techniques. The meaning of words changed. Some words dropped altogether out of daily use. They remained in Mark's text like verbal shells emptied of experiential associations. The events of Jesus' life and of the first apostolic years passed beyond the horizon of memory. Christians could no longer interpret Mark's account of the Gospel in light of their own recollection of Jesus and the first disciples.

There have always been exegetes in the Church to interpret the Gospel of Mark. Today's exegete is tributary of a tradition of interpretation which originated with Mark himself.

We may well be bewildered by the amount of scientific research already published on the Scriptures. We may be confused by the various kinds of research aimed at yielding the information now needed to understand them in their original context: historical criticism, form criticism, redaction criticism and literary criticism. Many conclusions may appear conflicting to us, while in reality they are complementary.

For many who have approached the Scriptures even with a superficial study, the exegetical challenge seems an insurmountable hurdle. The challenge is serious. Surely a basic understanding of Scripture in its original context is required of one who would use it for prayer. Hopefully, the day is at hand when all Christians will consider it normal to include the Scriptures in their education.

The extraordinary thing is not that we should feel the need to study the Scriptures. The early second-century author of 2 Peter found that Paul's writings contained some obscure passages. Mark felt the need to supply background information to clarify his message. Well before the time of Jesus, Jewish tradition had committed itself to the study of the Scriptures in order to draw inspiration for daily life and in view of synagogue prayer. Study is deeply inscribed in biblical tradition. What is truly extraordinary is that we have not all along given a due place to a field of study so intimately related to the root experiences of our religion.

Upon reflection, it should appear very normal to encounter difficulty in praying with a literary text we do not understand. It should also seem absolutely normal for a committed Christian to have more than a superficial knowledge of the origins of the Christian community to which he belongs

The exegetical challenge should not be exaggerated. Many unfortunately abandon use of the Scriptures in prayer because they have given up all hope of understanding them. There is no reason to think that we must understand a text thoroughly prior to praying with it. Who could claim such knowledge? The biblical scholar? Hardly! His study frequently does little more than deepen personal awareness of his ignorance.

Actually, there are few literary works that we read with full comprehension. We read and enjoy them with the understanding we have. Aware of our limitations, we spend many years studying literature. With our minds open to better understanding, we are careful in drawing conclusions from our reading. We would do well to approach the Scriptures in the same way. Confronting the exegetical challenge is not only a matter of study but of attitude. A balanced approach accepts limitations in understanding, while recognizing the need to learn.

Obviously, the more we know of the Scriptures, the better we can pray with them. It is possible, however, that someone with expert knowledge might have a very low quality of prayer, or even be entirely unable to pray. It is not sufficient to know what a Paul or a Luke meant when he wrote to the Christian communities of the first century. There are many factors involved, many challenges to genuine biblical prayer. Exegesis is but a preliminary challenge. To understand the Scriptures, we must first have discovered them in their origins.

Understanding the Scriptures

Do you still not see or comprehend?
—Mark 8:17

Exegesis is not the only intellectual challenge we face in turning to the Scriptures for prayer, unless of course we understand exegesis in its primitive general sense of narration or interpretation. Ancient exegesis was a two-pronged effort. First, the original setting in life of the Scriptures had to be discovered and explained. Second, the Scriptures had to be re-read in terms of another culture or moment of history. They needed to be translated not only from one language into another, but from one culture into another.

In earliest times, this second task of exegesis, now referred to as the art of hermeneutics, clearly predominated. Rightly so. Why would anyone have read the Scriptures apart from their contemporary meaningfulness? Unless biblical prayer can be experienced as our own prayer, as an expression of our personal religious attitude, praying with the Scriptures is a senseless exercise. The early Christians did not view the Bible as a literary museum piece, but as their Bible, as the abiding word of God addressed not only to ages past but to them. They considered the Gospels not so much as a story of what had happened, but as an explanation for what was happening. Their primary question was not "What did the text mean to its original intended readers?" but "What does it mean now?" and "How is it our prayer?"

The Question

Even when the original meaning of a term or passage is clear, it may still be difficult to use it for prayer. In John's Gospel, the expression "good shepherd" situates Christ in a matrix of religious relationships patterned on ancient social structures which no longer obtain. We may well understand the life-situation of a shepherd in first-century Palestine as well as its metaphorical application to the role of Christ. But even so, few of us are familiar enough with the life of a shepherd to consider it an apt metaphor for Christ's relationship to his followers. Many have never seen sheep, let alone a shepherd. The idea of sheep implies social subservience, hardly a viable relationship for men and women bent on Christian self-realization.

The question is obvious. How can we express the deeper reality expressed in the ancient metaphor in terms of our experience and contemporary personal and social attitudes? Failure to truly translate this expression saps its strength and reduces it to a romantic image having little to do with real life. The "good shepherd" becomes the spotless, white-robed, red-manteled figure of popular art. Staff in hand, he stands in a flowered field, a refuge from life's concerns. As spotless sheep, we gaze peacefully upwards into his clear-eyed and untroubled features. The "good shepherd" is no longer one who protects and guides us in the midst of life's activities. We turn to him rather to escape the troubles and preoccupations of life.

Much of the scientific work done on the Scriptures since the last century all but ignores this second and most vital dimension of exegesis. It is exegesis in the limited modern sense, which directs its efforts at uncovering the primitive context of biblical writings.

Recent studies have focused increasingly on the insufficiency of a purely historical approach to the Bible, however scientific. We are not those early Christians at Corinth. Our historical and sociological situation is vastly different from theirs. How then is a biblical work to be interpreted by the contemporary reader? What does it mean today? For biblical prayer, the answer is crucial.

Both types of study are essential. In Mark, for example, we found them extremely closely related. We may even wonder whether it is possible to grasp the original meaning of a word unless we have found a way to relate it adequately to our situation and experience. Conversely, how is it possible to convey an ancient expression in contemporary terms without first having discerned its primitive sense? At every step, the process is one of mutual clarification. The better we understand John's use of the expression "good shepherd", the more aptly can we translate it into living reality. As we gradually discover the contemporary implications of Christ's shepherding role, we are apt to exclaim, "Is that what John meant?" Only at this point does John's tenth chapter become a good vehicle for our personal prayer: "I am the good shepherd; I know my own sheep and my sheep know me" (10:14).

In modern terminology, no exegesis is possible without some measure of hermeneutics, and vice versa. Our attention may focus on one or other of these poles of interpretation, but the two cannot be divorced. The manner in which the ancients expressed both functions with the one term, exegesis, serves as an apt warning.

The Answer

The word hermeneutics also has its roots in antiquity. Like exegesis it referred to the entire reality of interpretation, and not to the one task of expressing an ancient work in contemporary terms as it does in its more limited modern sense. The Greek noun from which it was drawn, *hermeneutes,* meant translator or interpreter. The interpreter translated from one language into another. Like the narrator, his work resulted in a new interpretation of someone else's language. While the remote roots of exegesis lie in the art of the narrator and those of hermeneutics in that of the translator, the two were extremely closely related in that both were interpreters.

The word *hermeneutes* can be found in classical Greek literature, in the New Testament and in early Christian literature. Perhaps its best known ancient attestation is in a second century reference to Mark as the interpreter *(hermeneutes)* of Peter. Papias attributes the statement to an otherwise unknown personage named John the Elder. Precisely how Mark was the interpreter of Peter is unclear. Did he merely translate Peter's evangelical teaching and preaching from Aramaic into Greek? Did he adapt Peter's message to the life situation of a broader audience than had been Peter's? Is it that Mark's work, for all its individuality, is a reflection of Christian tradition as presented especially by Peter? Judging from the Gospel itself, it may be that not one of these alone, but all of them together represents a fair assessment of the evangelist's interpretative role.

The work of the hermeneut was called *hermeneia.* The term is widely attested in Greek philosophical works beginning with pre-Socratic times, in Hellenistic Greek and in papyri. It also appears in the Prologue to Sirach, a work which shows remarkable awareness of the problem of translation and interpretation:

> You therefore are now invited to read it [Sirach's translation] in a spirit of attentive good will, with indulgence for any apparent failure on our part, despite earnest efforts, in the interpretation *(hermeneia)* of particular passages. For words spoken originally in Hebrew are not as effective when they are translated into another language. That is true not only of this book but of the Law itself, the Prophets and the rest of the books, which differ no little when they are read in the original.

Sirach clearly perceived how as a translator he could not avoid personally interpreting the work of another. A translation is far more than the passage of a work from one language into another. With each sentence, the translator must judge personally how a work which had been written for another people could best be rendered for his potential readers. A good translation is a new literary creation. Witness, for example, Alexander Pope's poetic translation of the *Iliad* and the *Odyssey,* or more recently Herbert Mason's *Gilgamesh.* Fellini's film interpretation of *Satyricon* represents the creative genius of Fellini no less than that of Petronius.

Paul too was aware of the need for *hermeneia*, but in a different context: "One receives the gift of tongues, another that of interpreting *(hermeneia)* the tongues" (1 Cor. 12:10). Chapter 14 of the same letter deals at length with the problem of *hermeneia* in relation to the phenomenon of ecstatic language. In a community context, public prayer must be intelligent. Ecstatic utterance must be properly interpreted. Otherwise, it remains so much gibberish, talking into the air (1 Cor. 14:7-19). Paul's use of the term *hermeneia* was closely related to the function of the priest at Delphi who translated the unintelligible utterances of the oracle into a message which could be understood by the suppliant. This work of interpretation took place through the inspiration of Hermes, whose name may well stand at the origin of the term *hermeneia*.

In the Emmaus pericope, the dialogue between Jesus and the two disciples leads up to an important lesson in biblical hermeneutics. For the disciples' benefit, Jesus interpreted every passage in the Scriptures which referred to him (Luke 24:27). In so doing, he removed false expectations, revealed the meaning of sacred literature in a new context and prepared the disciples to recognize his presence in the breaking of the bread.

Upon examining but a few examples of the use of the terms *hermeneutes* and *hermeneia* we become aware of the breadth of the reality covered by these terms. The precise meaning varies with the nature of what is to be translated, the means invoked in translation and the audience for whom the translation is effected. As an aspect of communication, *hermeneia* cannot be restricted to mechanical translation, if this is at all possible. The term is rich with all the dimensions of an interpretation which brings someone to genuine understanding.

The term hermeneutics is then just as encompassing as exegesis. Like exegesis it confronts a biblical passage and seeks to make it understandable to the contemporary reader. It differs from exegesis in that it focuses specifically on the problem of actualizing the message. Its major concern is the present-day relevance of the message and not its primitive meaningfulness.

The Tradition

The development of New Testament interpretation was mainly a matter of hermeneutics. We saw this in the way Mark approached Christian tradition and in the manner Matthew and Luke utilized the Gospel according to Mark. It becomes even clearer in the patristic literature of the latter half of the second century, when the history of self-conscious interpretation of the canonical Gospels began.

The early Christians interpreted the Old Testament within the tradition of the rabbis. When they turned their attention to the literary works of the New Testament, they invoked the same methods. At Alexandria, which by the time of Jesus had become an exciting intellectual center for both Jew and Gentile, the thought climate was greatly influenced by Platonic philosophy with its emphasis on the way in which observable realities are but a mirror of the real world of ideas which is not directly perceivable. Such a philosophical milieu readily led to an allegorical interpretation of the Scriptures, which were part of the world of observable phenomena. Their hidden meaning had to be discovered. Philo, surely the most prominent of first-century intellectuals in the Jewish community of Alexandria, was the chief exponent of this method of interpretation.

When the first educated Alexandrian Christians interpreted Christian tradition, they did so within the intellectual tradition well established for the interpretation of the Old Testament. The manner in which this conflicted with Palestinian interpretation of tradition is reflected in the divisions in the church of Corinth occasioned by the teaching of an Alexandrian Christian named Apollos (1 Cor. 1:6). Many of the Greek Christians of Corinth found the wisdom of Alexandria far more palatable than the simple kerygmatic proclamation they had received from Paul.

As it became increasingly more difficult to relate the Gospel writings to the life of Alexandrian Christians, interpretation became more and more allegorical. Men like Clement of Alexandria and Origen searched the Gospels for hidden meaning. Literary works did not need to be considered in their entirety. Each word, phrase and passage had an allegorical meaning of its own.

The focus of Alexandrian interpretation was hermeneutical rather than exegetical. Informational background was not especially needed. Persons, places, things, words, phrases and entire passages all possessed an allegorical meaning which could be discovered through a process of personal introspection. Platonists considered such introspection to be but a calling to memory of ideas innate in the human psyche. Recourse to the original historical situation had little value. We can hardly quarrel with the intention of the great Alexandrian exponents of allegorical interpretation, which was to show the meaningfulness of the New Testament Scriptures. We can understand, however, how allegorical interpretation could often become completely gratuitous.

Alexandria was not the only school of Christian biblical interpretation. An equally important school arose at Antioch. In the latter part of the second century, while Clement and Origen emphasized allegorical interpretation at Alexandria, the Antiochene Theophilus was laying the foundations for a careful exegetical treatment of the traditional texts. The school and method of Antioch came to full prominence in the fourth and fifth centuries with Diodorus of Tarsus, Theodore of Mopsuestia and John Chrysostom. Reacting to Alexandrian methods of interpretation, these writers emphasized careful grammatical treatment of the text. They based their interpretation on precise literal meaning and on the relationship of each passage to its literary context.

Neither approach to the Gospels was exclusive. Origen did not totally ignore the literal sense. At times, he could be extremely perspicacious in discerning it. John Chrysostom did not overlook the possible allegorical meaning of the text especially where the text itself invited it. The allegorical tradition is rooted in the New Testament itself. Mark not only supplied historical information as an exegetical aid for his readers. He also transmitted the allegorical interpretation of Jesus' parable of the sower and the seed (4:3-20). Intellectually, Mark the interpreter was both an Antiochene and an Alexandrian.

From the contemporary point of view, it is obvious that Alexandrian interpretation was deficient in its appreciation of the historical situation of the New

Testament text, and that Antiochene interpretation frequently disregarded the relationship of the historical text to the situation of Antiochenes.

The Paradox

Paradoxically, the contemporary tendency towards literal interpretation in praying with the Scriptures most closely resembles the allegorizing of our Alexandrian forbears. Such interpretation is usually termed fundamentalist. It is based on the view that the Scriptures are God's word and consequently not subject to the contingencies of human history. It approaches the Scriptures as though they had been written in our own day, as though they should be readily understood without recourse to exegetical analysis of their literary nature and historical background. Given the change in culture and in the use of language from the first century to the twentieth, however, fundamentalist interpretation is frequently closer to pure allegory than to the literal meaning it claims to espouse. The literal meaning of the Bible is inseparable from the intention of its human authors.

At base, the greatest shortcoming of fundamentalist interpretation stems from its failure to grasp the truly human and historical quality of God's word. In speaking through human words, God speaks through particular human words, words which are symbolically meaningful and rich in personal and historical associations in their expression of what God means for man. God does not speak through intrinsically meaningless verbal mirrors of divine ideas which somehow become bearers of transcendent truth in their contemporary usage.

In fundamentalist interpretation, we are faced with a kind of biblical docetism. For the docetist, Christ only appeared to be a man; as Son of God, he could not truly be considered a human being. For the fundamentalist, the biblical word has but the appearance of a human word. As the transcendent word of God, it escapes the categories of human communication; its exegesis, however well-intentioned, is a desecration. If we accept John's proclamation that "the word was made flesh" (John 1:14), we cannot reject the human quality of all divine communication.

The hermeneutical challenge is basically one of discovering how a text which reflected an ancient culture also mirrors our own. It is a matter of translating a response to a particular historical situation into a response to our own situation. Hermeneutics deals with the problem of contemporary meaningfulness and relevance. A work written in one social context must be interpreted in terms of another.

Hermeneutics requires a good understanding of a work in its original setting as well as a good understanding of the present moment of history, and of the personal, social and religious conditions which now obtain. It demands sensitivity to the symbolic functions of language. Must we all be theologians to use the Scriptures for prayer? No more than we need be professional exegetes.

All of us engage in hermeneutics. We constantly are called upon to express the meaning of historical events in terms of our experience. The newspaper reporter is a hermeneut. So is the husband who returns home and tells his wife what happened that day at work. Every time we present someone else's literary creation in our own words, we engage in hermeneutics. Whenever we read aloud to someone, we interpret a text with our intonation, our pauses, our pace and our emphases. Public reading is an exercise in hermeneutics. So is the direction of a play and the interpretation of a song. Every effort to explain something for another's benefit is an attempt at hermeneutics.

We may not realize it, but whenever we personally pray with the Scriptures, we engage in biblical hermeneutics. We may well smile at finding ourselves in the position of Molière's Monsieur Jourdan, thrilling at the discovery that from his earliest years he actually had spoken in prose.

The quality of popular hermeneutics varies a great deal. Yet, we do not require that someone possess an expert's understanding of his historical situation before he ventures an interpretation. We simply recognize normal limitations. In the same way, no one should be put off from praying with the Scriptures on the basis of his inexpertise at hermeneutics. The challenge of hermeneutics is basically one of awareness. As in the case of exegesis, acceptance of limitations and openness to better understanding are all that are required.

The Challenge of Life

And so man became a living being.

—Gen. 2:7

The Scriptures stood before us like a vast literary monument, cold and lifeless, a sphinx, a pyramid, a rock-hewn tomb in the Valley of Kings, a sacred precinct. We gazed upon the stylized features of its heroes, wondering what had brought us here. Was this really a place for us? We felt as midgets in a land of giants.

Was it a smile we discerned on those mysterious stone colossi of biblical history or a striking play of light, a subtle shadow? Why were we unable to leave? Had we been recognized? We thought we heard the muffled sound of God's word. Did we belong? For a long time, we stood there, unable to run, afraid of being overwhelmed.

What meant this fascination? There was life here, after all these centuries, but could we bear it? Should we enter? Dare we greet Abraham? What would he say to us? We might be destroyed by our own echo.

Yet we dared. We entered, or we thought we did. Exegesis. Hermeneutics. We explored the ancient monument. We crossed its courts, penetrated its hidden passages, traced its reliefs and scrambled over its heights. We measured ourselves against its obelisks and saw our reflection in its sacred pools. The excitement of discovery. History. Poetry. Knowledge. Wisdom. But is this prayer? Has God's word been made mere grammar or theological literature for us? Have we really greeted Abraham? Did we present ourselves to him as sensitive human beings or as human derivatives which staff the universe of "ologies"?

Curators in a well-ordered museum, we leave for home once our day's work is done. Do exegetes and hermeneuts really pray? Have they the eyes to see? Have they the ears to hear?

The challenge is greater than we had imagined. How can we appreciate the word of biblical life if we have not lived? The problem lies not so much with the Scriptures as with our inability to face life, with our reluctance to live it. How can we hope to hear God's word if we ourselves have not accepted divine life, if we have not become a living word of God? Study may be indispensable. In no way is it adequate. How can we pray with the Scriptures without participating in biblical experience? Ezekiel did not read the scroll; he ate it (Ez. 3:3). Paul did not view the fight or attend the race. He finished the race. He fought a good fight (2 Tim. 4:7).

The experiential challenge is more critical than the intellectual. To pray with the Scriptures, we must share in some measure in the life experiences, and especially in the experience of God, which underlie the biblical word. The Old and New Testaments reflect every aspect of a richly lived life in its religious dimension. They express a people's faith encounter with God. Apart from a life fully lived and a faith truly personal, biblical prayer devolves into a sad and empty exercise, a sound, no longer a word. We should not attribute to limited knowledge what in reality springs from lack of faith or shallow escapist living. Life and faith, these are the ultimate roots of genuine biblical prayer, as of all true prayer. We thought we had penetrated the Scriptures. We had only begun to prepare.

Reflecting on the great Mesopotamian Epic of Gilgamesh, Herbert Mason wrote: "It is, after all, a story that is understood immediately by anyone who has suffered loss, a loss one has yearned to restore and finally has had to accept." Mason himself had shared the experience of Gilgamesh in the loss of a very close friend who succumbed to Hodgkin's disease. Generalizing from his experience, he would have all of us read Gilgamesh with experiential understanding.

> Deaths due to war or other acts involving human morality in some discernible way must be opposed and to some extent can be and are; but a death which has no apparent relation to morality leaves the survivor, if he loved the one who died, helpless and half-crazed, trying to explain, understand, protest, reverse the gratuitous, or reenter the real world with some trace of the old normalcy that has been lost... We lost the one who we didn't realize enabled us to live in other people's worlds; now we have only our own private world and the almost herculean task of constructing a human reentry. What we finally do, out of desperation to recover the sense of the "outside," is to go on an impossible, or even forbidden, journey or pilgrimage, which from a rational point of view is futile: to find the one wise man, whomever or wherever he may be...; and to find from him the secret of

> eternal life or the secret of adjusting to this life as best we can.[1]

Gilgamesh was but one work. The Bible is an entire literature. There is hardly a shade of the experiential spectrum which does not find expression in its pages. The scriptural accounts are the literary creation of extraordinary men, of men who have truly lived, of men who loved, hoped, struggled, feared, failed and suffered, of men who exulted in the presence of God and suffered at his remoteness. They reflect the experience of men who passed through the purification of life and emerged whole and renewed, men who unravelled the complexities of human existence and arrived at mature simplicity.

The Bible is the story of human life. We should not be distracted by its ancient Near Eastern or its Hellenistic and Roman trappings. Cleared of its Mediterranean staging and stripped of its exotic garb, it is the story of life itself, naked and classical, every man's life. It is a story that can be understood immediately by anyone who has lived.

Have we thrilled at the sight of dawn, at new light dispelling the night's shadows, defining the horizon, giving to everyone and everything its place in a luminous world? Then we shall understand the first morning of Genesis when the earth was a formless wasteland and darkness covered the abyss, until God said: "Let there be light" (1:1-3).

Have we yearned for absolute independence, for unlimited knowledge, for total creative dominion over the universe and even our own destiny? Have we refused to accept our personal human limitations?

[1] Herbert Mason, *Gilgamesh, A Verse Narrative.* Boston, Houghton Mifflin Company, Boston, p. 100.

Have we desired to be like God? Have we felt the shame, the confusion, the aloneness, the alienation, the inner death which springs from our refusal to be ourselves? Then we shall grasp Genesis' story of man and woman, reaching out from their garden oasis, snatching at the divine order of wisdom only to find banishment in a world suddenly inhospitable (Gen. 2:4–3:24).

Have we looked on our brother's accomplishments with envy, trapped in an inner struggle to assert our own self-worth? Have we struck out at him in anger, in a misdirected effort to find peace? Have we killed his personal development with silence? Murder can be so subtle. Have we felt the fear and experienced the restless spiritual wandering of one who has killed? Then we shall understand the story of Cain and Abel (Gen. 4:1-16).

Have we feared the destructive forces of nature, the storm, the unfettered sea, the drought, the earthquake? Have we seen the evil of man's own making, the wars, the bombings, the pollution, the slums, the addictions? Have we known the precariousness of life? Then we shall understand the story of the flood, of evil waters which would destroy all order and reduce the earth to the formless waste from which it was created (Gen. 6:5–9:17).

Have we shared man's ambition to build the city? Have we felt his all-sufficiency, his need to make a name for himself? Have we tasted the disillusionment of success, aloneness in company, inability to communicate with those about us? The story of Babel and its presumptuous tower will not be a mystery to us (Gen. 11:1-9).

Have we struggled in interior darkness to emerge into the light of renewed hope through the personal warmth and support of a fellow human being? We can then appreciate how whatever came to be in the eternal Word found life, life for the light of men, how that light shines on in unconquering darkness, "the real light enlightening every man", the Word become flesh (John 1:4-5, 9, 14). "Here begins the gospel of Jesus Christ, the Son of God" (Mark 1:1).

Have we felt a thirst which no water could quench, a hunger which no bread could satisfy? How then shall we fail to recognize the living water of Christ, a water which dissolves all thirst to become a fountain within us, leaping up to provide eternal life (John 4:4-15)? How shall we turn away from the bread of life, an all-satisfying, imperishable food, given unto life eternal (John 6:25-59)?

As we approach the Scriptures for prayer, we bring varying degrees of experience. Rarely, if ever, do we possess the entire range of experience reflected in biblical experience, or even in the experiential substratum of a single passage. To use the Scriptures for prayer, we must have shared at least to a certain extent in the experience they narrate or presuppose.

It may be that the biblical text clearly mirrors our conscious experience. Very often, however, it will draw what until now remained hidden and unconscious into the light consciousness. The great covenant texts will give us the sense of personal value that we lack: "I shall be your God, and you will be my people." Secure in our self-worth, we shall be able to confront areas of life and past experience which until now have been too painful for us to face. As in a genuine love-experience, we shall have the courage to be ourselves. The historical writings which sparked our self-acceptance will become more meaningful as we progressively allow our genuine experience to surface. The prophets will then enable us to face the personal and social responsibilities we have long shunned. The sages will show us how to live in the face of contradictions, suffering, illness and even death. No longer shall we fear. We shall discover our growing commitment to life reflected in the Scriptures.

The Scriptures may also expand our experience into regions heretofore unfamiliar. They will give rise to new experience by extending our acquired experience into analogous areas. Much depends on our willingness to grow in experiential knowledge, to assume responsibility for our own life education, and to turn to the Scriptures as a mediating tool, much as we would turn to a parent, a teacher or a friend.

Perhaps we have never undergone the purifying and liberating experience of a physical desert, the depth of self-confrontation it brings about, the realization it engenders of life's truly basic realities and of genuine human needs, the values of human openness it elicits. But then we may have felt deprivation, been reduced to essentials by inability to fulfill overambitious goals, or enjoyed a simple life in the course of a vacation or retreat. If ever we have pulled aside for a moment of reflection, putting life's complexity out of mind, we have tasted something of the desert. Turning to the biblical exodus and the experience of Sinai we may extend and deepen that experience and come to a new realization of our radical dependence and freedom as creatures among creatures. Fresh water will become a blessing, a piece of bread and human fellowship a priceless gift. We shall have learned to listen and respect. As we grow in our very humanity, the biblical desert will come to life for us.

The Bible's mature reflection on experience leads us to reflect on our own experience. It addresses the reader directly. "Son of man stand up! I wish to speak with you" (Ez. 2:1). Already it is too late to escape.

There are questions.

> Who is this that obscures divine plans
> with words of ignorance?
> Gird up your loins now, like a man;
> I will question you, and you tell me the answers!
> (Job 38:2-3).

The questions are pointed. They lead to new and better formulations of experience.

> Where were you when I founded the earth?
> Tell me, if you have understanding (Job 38:4).
>
> Have you ever in your lifetime commanded the
> morning and shown the dawn its place
> For taking hold of the ends of the earth,
> till the wicked are shaken from its surface?
> (Job 38:12-13).
>
> Will we have arguing with the Almighty by the
> critic?
> Let him who would correct God give answer!
> (Job 40:2).

Job's question was an experiential one. God's answer was equally experiential. With a new realization of his actual relationship to God and the created universe, Job responded:

> I know that you can do all things,
> and that no purpose of yours can be hindered
> (42:2).
>
> I had heard of you by word of mouth,
> but now my eye has seen you (42:5).

To pray with the Scriptures we must accept to be challenged. Job, every one of us, the Scriptures constantly shake us loose from our inadequate self-concepts, our unfounded assumptions and our facile judgments of what reality must be.

Perhaps the course of events appears senseless to us. We find ourselves in the company of Paul, anguished at the fact that his fellow Jews had not accepted Christ.

> I speak the truth in Christ: I do not lie. My conscience bears me witness in the Holy Spirit that there is great grief and constant pain in my heart. Indeed, I could even wish to be separated from Christ for the sake of my brothers, my kinsmen the Israelites. Theirs were the adoption, the glory, the covenants, the law-giving, the worship, and the promises; theirs were the patriarchs and from them came the Messiah (I speak of his human origins) (Rom. 9:1-5).

With Paul we try to discern meaning in history, aware that all may never be clear to us: "Blessed forever be God who is over all! Amen" (Rom. 9:5).

Our expectations may have been shattered. "We were hoping that he (Jesus of Nazareth) was the one who would set Israel free" (Luke 24:21). With the disciples of Emmaus we may come to recognize the Lord in the breaking of the bread.

Biblical answers become our answers once biblical questions have become our questions. Peter's "You are the Messiah" means little to us until we too have confronted Jesus' question: "Who do people say that I am?" Who is Jesus? Is he John the Baptizer? Elijah? One of the prophets? Even after Peter's messianic proclamation, we continue to ask: "Who is Jesus?" We do so because we know Jesus personally and experientially. We do so in the knowledge that we can never fully say who he is. We accept this limitation out of respect for his personal mystery. The Scriptures may enable us to formulate an answer. But we know that they can never be fully successful, for ultimately the question is a personal one. Who is Jesus for us? The answer, even when biblically formulated, must also be personal.

Some Scripture texts obviously coincide with our experience better than others. A passage may be especially meaningful because it reflects our present state of soul or level of maturity. We should pray with passages which speak to us. Yes, we may be extremely limited, but then not every work or passage expresses the full range of biblical experience.

As we engage in life and are enriched by experience, the biblical word becomes more meaningful to us. Each re-reading brings new understanding. We recall earlier biblical reading, aware that even then our unrecognizing hearts were burning within us as God spoke to us along the way. We wonder how it is that we could have missed so much. Until now the Scriptures had little resonance in our experience. Not the Scriptures, but our experience of life was lacking. An intense experience should find us in the position of Viktor Frankl, spontaneously repeating the same biblical prayer.

> One day, a few days after the liberation, I walked through the country past flowering meadows, for miles and miles, toward the market town near the camp. Larks rose to the sky and I could hear their joyous song. There was no one to be seen for miles around; there was nothing but the wide earth and sky and the larks' jubilation and the freedom of space. I stopped, looked around, and up to the sky—and then I went down on my knees. At that

> moment there was very little I knew of myself or of the world—I had but one sentence in mind—always the same: 'I called to the Lord from my narrow prison and He answered me in the freedom of space.'
>
> How long I knelt there and repeated this sentence memory can no longer recall. But I know that on that day, in that hour, my new life started. Step for step I progressed, until I again became a human being.[1]

It is not the Bible but we who were dead. Ours to come to life, to become human. Even now, we have only begun to grow. As our life takes substance, we can expect ever sharper focus from its biblical reflection. The Bible is a museum only for those who would make it such. For us who would pray with the Scriptures, it must be home.

[1] Viktor E. Frankl, *Man's Search for Meaning*. New York, Washington Square Press, 1963, pp. 141-142.

Experience of God

You are my intimate friend.
—Exod. 33:12

Experience of life attunes us to the Scriptures. As the Bible keeps pace with our broadening experience, we never cease to be amazed at its perceptiveness. No one outgrows the classical literature of Jewish and Christian origins.

But the Bible is no mere human literature. Its expressiveness, its ideational content and its evocativeness are the human expression of God's word. Even stripped of its divine dimension, the Bible remains experientially one of the richest literary collections ever assembled. For all of its literary value, however, only faith can transform it into a vehicle of prayer.

Without faith, the Bible is like a religious painting, an El Greco, a Fra Angelico or a Rembrandt, which is approached without the artist's faith inspiration. It remains a masterwork of human achievement, a piece of artistic creativity which no humanist can ignore. Its aesthetic quality is undeniable. Even so, its essential dimension is missing.

Given all of El Greco's technical skill, and with all of his deeply felt experience of life, no one could reproduce his effort without likewise sharing in his religious spirit. Such work would have been shorn of its spiritual dynamism, emptied of its soul. In no way would it approach a genuine El Greco.

The most fundamental inspiration governing Fra Angelico's work was divine. God revealed himself in the artist's faith experience. When the Florentine friar embodied his faith in a work of art, he gave visual expression to the depths of his religious being and to God's personal self-revelation to him. Aesthetic creativity and religious inspiration joined to produce one artistic work which was both human and divine. Fra Angelico's work was divine Being communicated in human art.

Everyone who truly appreciates a work of Rembrandt reproduces and recreates it in the depths of his person. His soul becomes the mirror of the art work before him. He communicates, he becomes one, with the artist's work at the experiential levels of his personality. As he recreates it in contemplation, he gradually discovers it, just as the artist himself had discovered his work in the process of creating it. Without a religious experience analogous to that of the artist, however, he communicates with but a limited aspect of it. He reduces the work to the flatness of his own one-dimensional experience. The depth is gone. Only the painted surface remains. A religious person, and only a religious person, can appreciate the true dimensions of Rembrandt's art.

The same is true of biblical literature. Think of Job, with its vision of man sweeping the heavens.

> Have you fitted a curb to the Pleiades,
> or loosened the bonds of Orion?
> Can you bring forth the Mazzaroth in their season,
> or guide the Bear with its train? (38:31-32).

Consider Isaiah's dream of man at peace in the rule of Emmanuel.

> Then the wolf shall be a guest of the lamb,
> and the leopard shall lie down with the kid;
> The calf and the young lion shall browse together,
> with a little child to guide them.
> The cow and the bear shall be neighbors,
> together their young shall rest;
> the lion shall eat hay like the ox.
> The baby shall play by the cobra's den,
> and the child lay his hand on the adder's lair
> (11:6-8).

Surely the work of Job and Isaiah stand among the very best literature ever to be produced by man. For another time, language and culture, their work is worthy of Homer, Virgil, Shakespeare and Dante. Our human experience will never exhaust its human quality. Little dare we hope to mirror it in our experience or personally recreate it adequately. Even on the purely human level, we may never fully communicate with the works of these giants of Hebrew literature.

Our limitations, however, may be far more than human. Without the religious experience which animated Job and Isaiah, our efforts will be frustrated from the start. To truly grow with them, to share in their inspiration, even in an incipient way, we must share in the experience of God they mean to express. The work of Job and Isaiah is not only classical literature; it is God's word classically expressed. It is classical prayer.

> Behold, I am of little account; what can I answer you?
> I put my hand over my mouth.
> Though I have spoken once, I will not do so again;
> though twice, I will do so no more (Job 40:4-5).

> Let justice descend, O heavens, like dew from above,
> like gentle rain let the skies drop it down.
> Let the earth open and salvation bud forth;
> let justice also spring up!
> I, the Lord, have created this (Is. 45:8).

To appreciate these works, we must not only have tasted life, we must be able to pray.

Biblical literature expresses a personal relationship with God. To enter into its spirit, to enjoy it, to really read it, we must share in this same relationship. The biblical word projects us out of its pages towards a greater life experience of union with God. Communication with biblical literature is communication with God.

Genuine reading is not a state of passive receptivity, but a conscious activity, a new creation, the reincarnation of a literary work. In the case of the Scriptures, that activity is prayer. God's biblical word resounds in our very act of praying. We cannot truly read the Scriptures without praying them. We otherwise miss their most basic intentionality. Without a sounding box, we pluck at strings drawn over a simple board. The words are hollow. The words are empty. In no way do they speak to us.

We must not think of prayer as a divine address to be followed by a human response. Like the early Christians awaiting a historical return of Christ, we should wait a long time for such a word of address. God addresses us in our response. Already Christ was present in the Christian community. It was their responsibility to grow in their relationship to Christ and thereby increase his sacramental presence.

God's word is heard in our own human word. As we pray, God's word grows in both clarity and intensity for us and, through us, for others.

Surely, we may express our relationship with God as a dialogue. That is the manner of human communication. But in reality, God's address and our response are one. Their unity is clear from a consideration of the Psalms, whose literary nature is that of a response to God in prayer. The same Psalms, however, are also the record of God's word to us. The record is actualized and God's word is heard when we pray the Psalms, when we address God with their classic formulations of our most basic attitudes of prayer. To read the Psalms, the psalmist's "Hearken, O God, to my prayer" (Ps. 55:2) must be a personal plea. The same is true of the Our Father. If we are to hear Matthew's word, Luke's word, God's word, in the Our Father, we must pray it and not merely read it as we would another work. To really read the Our Father is to pray the Our Father.

The Scriptures do not constitute a magical key to the house of prayer. Nor do they transform an empty house into a home. No one can reasonably expect that the Scriptures will make him pray or that they will transform a non-prayerful attitude into a prayerful one. They may help to evoke a prayerful response to God's presence. They may enable us to formulate our prayer. But they cannot supply for the lack of a fundamental disposition to pray. To expect otherwise can only engender disappointment and frustration. A truism? Perhaps. But do we not tend to avoid the most obvious? We seek deep reasons and learned explanations to account for our inabilities and inadequacies. We intellectualize our experiential problems. The answer is usually right at hand, intellectually simple, experientially uncompromising. Experiential difficulties can only by resolved experientially.

To pray with the Scriptures, we must first recognize our fundamental, radical, personal dependence on God. Psalm 86 may help us to realize the ramifications of such an attitude. Sensitive to his creaturely need, the psalmist prays:

> Incline your ear, O Lord; answer me,
> for I am afflicted and poor.
> Keep my life, for I am devoted to you:
> save your servant who trusts in you.
> You are my God; have pity on me, O Lord
> for to you I call all the day (vv. 1-3).

Aware of his accountability for a human life graciously granted him by God, he pleads:

> Gladden the soul of your servant,
> for to you, O Lord, I lift up my soul;
> For you, O Lord, are good and forgiving,
> abounding in kindness to all who call upon you (vv. 4-5).

Conscious of his obligation to accept a responsible role in history, he asks:

> Teach me, O Lord, your way
> that I may walk in your truth;
> direct my heart that it may fear your name (v. 11).

Turning to God as universal creator, source of life and Lord of history, he proclaims:

> There is none like you among the gods, O Lord,
> and there are no works like yours.
> All the nations you have made shall come
> and worship you, O Lord,
> and glorify your name.
> For you are great, and you do wondrous deeds;
> you alone are God (vv. 8-10).

Grateful to God, who ultimately fulfills his needs, he sings:

> I will give thanks to you, O Lord my God,
> with all my heart,
> and I will glorify your name forever.
> Great has been your kindness toward me;
> you have rescued me from the depths of the netherworld (vv. 12-13).

The presence of God is the critical element in this attitude of radical dependence. God was present. There was no need to prove his existence. Only "the fool says in his heart, 'There is no God' " (Ps. 14:1; 53:2).

How different this is from our own attitude, in which all must be subject to proof. All? Well, nearly all. We do not try to prove the existence of those we love. We do not spread them out before us to analyze them scientifically, objectively. Rational dissection is a profanation of love. We simply love them. We love them because we know them. We know them because they know us, because we have allowed them to know us, because we are present to them and they to us.

Love is an act of mutual presence, in which new life is born. Love sees with new eyes. It hears with new ears. It gives new life to thought, feeling, gestures, silence and words. Perhaps those who love have less need to prove everything. The experiential knowledge of love accepts the existence of people and things.

For biblical man, every experience of life was an experience of God. The universe was transparent with God's presence. "Since the creation of the world, invisible realities, God's eternal power and divinity have become visible, recognized through the things he has made" (Rom. 1:20). He it is who fixed the earth on firm foundations, who covered the land with an ocean garment, and raised the mountains high above the watery depths. He sends springs winding through mountain watercourses, giving every living thing to drink, raising bread from the moist earth and wine to gladden men's hearts (Ps. 104:1-18). Everywhere God is present. Nowhere can man escape. Might he perhaps flee to the heavens? God is there. To the netherworld, to the wings of dawn, to the limits of the sea, or into the darkness? Always God is there (Ps. 139:7-12). His voice is in the unleashed fury of the storm, thundering over the waters, breaking the cedars, striking fiery flames, shaking the desert, twisting the oaks and stripping the forests bare (Ps. 29).

Creation is man's universal meeting place with God. In communion with the divine artist's every work, man recreates the universe. Humanized by the human spirit, creation, the new creation in the Spirit of God, expresses man's presence to God, no less than God's presence to man. In the things which he has made, God calls out to man and man responds. In the heavens, on the earth and in the ocean depths, divine address and human response are one.

All things speak the praises of the Lord. Praise the Lord, you sun and moon, you shining stars, you highest heavens and even you waters above the heavens. Let the earth, the sea monsters and the depths, let the fire, the hail, the snow, the mist, and the storm winds, let the mountains and the hills, the fruit trees and the cedars, the wild beasts, the tame animals, the creeping things and the winged fowl, let all creation praise the Lord (Ps. 148:3-10).

God was also present in history, in each successive moment of man's continuous creation, in the whole of Israel's community history. Every happening was significant with God's intervention. Each event, from the call of Abraham to the Christian proclamation of the good news, was at once human and divine.

There were special events in which God's presence was particularly evident. For Israel to discover living water after a long trek through the desert when nearly all had despaired of life, surely this was one of God's wonders. For Israel to find nourishment in an endless wasteland when hope had all but died, clearly this was a sign of God's special presence. For Israel to vanquish an enemy when the assault seemed overwhelming, obviously this was one of God's great saving deeds. For Jesus to have risen to new life, here was an irrepressible sign of God's presence to his people. Such were the divine signs and wonders ever accompanying Israel from slavery into freedom, from fragmentation to community, from sin and death to life in God.

For Israel and the early Christians, the whole of history unfolded as the fulfillment of God's promise to be present to his people. Biblical history was the story of God's fidelity to his promise. It was also the story of Israel's effort to respond to God's commitment with its own fidelity. The history of the old and new Israel was a divine history, the story of a people sharing God's life in a covenant relationship: I will be your God, present to you in each event of history; and you shall be my people, present to me in each of those same events. Every saving event was a sign of mutual presence: we shall be present to one another.

God's presence in history included his presence in Israel's historical word. As living history was reflected upon and shared at Israel's gathering places and finally recorded in biblical literature, the reflection, the sharing and the record took their own place in Israel's history, to reinforce the memory of God's promise, to be consulted for light and inspiration. Of Jesus' birth, Matthew would say that "All this happened to fulfill what the Lord had said through the prophet" (Matthew 1:22). In his home synagogue at Nazareth, Jesus would present himself as the fulfillment of Isaiah's prophecy:

> The spirit of the Lord is upon me;
> therefore he has anointed me.
> He has sent me to bring glad tidings to the poor
> to proclaim liberty to captives,
> Recovery of sight to the blind
> and release to prisoners,
> To announce a year of favor from the Lord
> (Luke 4:18-19; Is. 61:1-2).

"Today this Scripture passage is fulfilled in your hearing" (Luke 4.21). From Jerusalem to the ends of the earth, the apostles would proclaim the events of Jesus' death and resurrection as "in accordance with the Scriptures" (1 Cor. 15.3-5; Acts 1:8).

Historical Faith

My father was a wandering Aramean.
—Deut. 26:5

Every generation tends to view itself as the beginning of significant history. Every generation is a new generation, a new genesis. Each of us was born on the sixth day, fully mature, needing only to find a companion and to organize the universe. But a few days prior to our birth, "the earth was a formless wasteland and darkness covered the abyss, while a mighty wind swept over the waters" (Gen. 1:2). Five days were devoted to prepare a vast arena as a suitable living space for us.

In a way, we are right. Each generation, each human being is a recapitulation of cosmological, organismic and human history. And yet, each one, past and present, is the product of the past. We are right, if we remember that every past generation was also a new genesis. Our originality is but a point in a long historical continuum, throbbing with life in the present, but created by the historical experience of countless generations. Its very uniqueness witnesses to the vitality of human tradition.

From a certain point of view, maturity may be viewed as the ability to situate oneself historically. In this respect, our biblical forbears were mature.

They saw faith as a reality of the present, as man's personal experiential knowledge of God in the actual moment, but they formulated their faith in terms of a long historical experience of God. They rejected both the blindness of an absolutized present and the sclerosis of a canonized past. Forever seeking to bridge the chasm of time, they succeeded in expressing their faith in biblical formulations. They viewed revelation as an historical present: God has (present) spoken (past) to his people. They asserted their faith within a tradition.

Biblical man's past success is our present challenge. The Bible has much to teach us on the art of contributing our uniqueness to the continuum of history. Learning from biblical experience, we too can pray with the Scriptures.

Historical Consciousness

Throughout the centuries of biblical history, Israelites, Jews and Christians identified with Abraham, Isaac and Jacob.

> My father was a wandering Aramean, who went down to Egypt with a small household and lived there as an alien. But there he became a nation great, strong and numerous. When the Egyptians maltreated and oppressed us, imposing hard labor upon us, we cried to the Lord, the God of our fathers, and he heard our cry and saw our affliction, our toil and our oppression. He brought us out of Egypt with his strong hand and outstretched arm, with terrifying power, with signs and wonders; and bringing us into this country, he gave us this land flowing with milk and honey (Deut. 26:5-9).

Each individual prayed in the consciousness of his personal identity. This was his prayer. He began in the first person singular: "*My* father." He also prayed in awareness of his personal relationship to Abraham, a relationship which spanned centuries of generations. Abraham was his *father.* He viewed Abraham as an individual person: "a wandering Aramean who went down to Egypt with a small household," but also as one who lived in the family community which sprang from him.

Abraham was one with his descendants: "There he became a nation great, strong and numerous." This solidarity of Abraham with future generations is what grounded each Israelite's relationship to his remote ancestor. He too, no less than the Hebrews in Egypt, was a son of Abraham.

The Israelite was not alone in his solidarity with Abraham. He saw himself as the member of a community, as belonging to a people, Abraham's historical and actual family. The prayer continues in the first person plural: "When the Egyptians maltreated and oppressed *us*... *we* cried to the Lord... and bringing us into *this* country, he gave us *this* land."

The experience of Abraham and the ancestors was Israel's history. Every Israelite who professed his faith in this ancient deuteronomic prayer viewed the days in Egypt, the deliverance from oppression and the entry into the promised land as part of his personal community experience. Heir to a land flowing with milk and honey, he situated himself in one historical continuum with Abraham, Isaac and Jacob and proceeded to make his offering: "Therefore, I have now brought you the first-fruits of the products of the soil which you, O Lord, have given me" (Deut. 26:10).

In the New Testament, Paul takes a similar attitude. He first sums up the history of the Christ event as presented in traditional credal formulae:

> That Christ died for our sins in accordance with the Scriptures; that he was buried and, in accordance with the Scriptures, rose on the third day; that he was seen by Cephas, then by the Twelve (1 Cor. 15:3-5).

Each event was unique: Christ died, he was buried, he rose, he was seen by this one person or by that group. These events, however, were not unrelated to Israel's past history. They were "in accordance with the Scriptures." Moreover, Christ's death had an intentionality which encompassed all Christians. He "died for our sins." His resurrection reached out to his followers. "He was seen."

Paul then drew the line of that historical continuum to the point where he could insert himself within it.

> After that he was seen by five hundred brothers at once, most of whom are still alive, although some have fallen asleep. Next he was seen by James; then by all the apostles. Last of all he was seen by me, as one born out of the normal course (1 Cor. 15:6-8).

These verses did not merely constitute Paul's early preaching to the Christians of Corinth. They were also his personal, prayerful profession of faith. The "our sins" included Paul's sins. He too had seen the risen Lord. The death, the burial, the resurrection and the appearances of Christ were part of his history. Had Paul not situated himself in that history, in no way could it have expressed his faith in prayer. He might have quoted from its formulations. He could not have prayed them.

The degree to which we view ourselves as part of that same history, which now encompasses several millennia, is one of the attitudinal keys to biblical prayer. The history which opened with Abraham did not end with Jesus' resurrection or with his appearance to Paul. It extends down to our own time to include us in its long continuum. We pray with the Scriptures, because like biblical men and women before us, we identify with the history formulated in its pages. Unless we too can say "*My* father was a wandering Aramean," and "Christ died for *our* sins," and "he was seen by *me*," meaning not Paul, but ourselves, we shall not be able to pray with the Scriptures.

The Historical Presence of God

The bond or unifying factor of biblical history was the guiding presence of God. Without his presence, there would have been not one history, but many histories, the ancient histories of diverse men and women, of various tribes and nations. David's assault on Jerusalem would have had little to do with Abraham's departure from Haran. Paul's mission to the Gentiles and the history of Jerusalem's royal house would have had nothing in common. Unity sprang from biblical history's relationship to one God, whose loving mercy endures forever (cf. Ps. 136).

Consider the text of the vocation of Moses: "I am the God of your father, the God of Abraham, the God of Isaac, the God of Jacob" (Exod. 3:6). Abraham, Isaac, Jacob and Moses were united in their religious relationship to one God, present to them at different historical periods. Without this relationship, we might speak of the history of Abraham, the history of Isaac, the history of Jacob and the history of Moses. By reason of this relationship, however, some six hundred years of history, reflecting vastly different cultural situations have been united into one single history.

In the tenth century B.C., the first major biblical writer, an author now known as the Yahwist, witnessed to the same traditional source of historical unity when he made of God the protagonist of Israel's epic history. Unlike the other great epics of antiquity, no single individual was selected as the key figure of history. Rather, several major figures extending across many centuries were united under the leadership of God himself. To the extent that the work of the Yahwist can be called an epic, it is a divine epic.

The same common relationship to God underlies the genealogical tables of the first nine chapters of Chronicles and makes of them a summary presentation of Israel's unique history. In the New Testament, Matthew included all of Hebrew and Israelite history in a sweeping summary statement of the genealogy of Jesus: "A family record of Jesus Christ, son of David, son of Abraham" (Matthew 1:1). Luke utilized the same technique in a bold statement which unites all men from Adam to Jesus in their sonship of God: "When Jesus began his work he was about thirty years of age, being — so it was supposed — the son of Joseph, son of Heli... son of Enos, son of Seth, son of Adam, son of God" (Luke 3:23, 38). In the prologue to his Gospel, John united all who were begotten of God (1:12-13) to the Word of God which was in the beginning (1:1) and through whom all things came into being (1:3).

Divine history did not cease with the death of the apostles. Like Paul, we must draw the line of history's continuum to our own point of insertion. Our religious history includes Ignatius of Antioch facing martyrdom, Irenaeus upholding Christian tradition, Augustine confronting world crisis with the *City of God,* Jerome patiently translating the Scriptures in his Bethlehem cave, Thomas Aquinas placing the wisdom of Greece and the learning of Islam at the service of Christian faith, Thomas More living his religious conviction unto death, Marie-Joseph Lagrange humbly and courageously pursuing biblical truth in spite of official suspicion. These too are "our fathers." They too are Christians who saw the risen Lord. United in one history by a common relationship to God in Christ, they are inscribed in our theological genealogy. Their history, along with that of countless others, is our history.

The Arena of Creation

Biblical man sank his historical roots in the created universe.

> When I behold your heavens, the work of your fingers,
> the moon and the stars which you set in place —
> What is man that you should be mindful of him;
> or the son of man that you should care for him?
> You have made him little less than the angels,
> and crowned him with glory and honor.
> You have given him rule over the works of your hands,
> putting all things under his feet:
> All sheep and oxen,
> yes, and the beasts of the field,

The birds of the air, the fishes of the sea,
and whatever swims the paths of the seas
(Ps. 8:4-9).

Like the psalmist, early biblical writers such as the Yahwist and the Priestly Writer situated history in the context of creation. For them, the unity of history manifested that of the entire universe in its relationship to God. Creation and history were so interrelated that each single moment of history represented a spark of creation.

Other peoples like the Sumerians, the Babylonians and the Egyptians had long developed the classical myths of creation. The Israelites drew upon these and reinterpreted them in terms of their own experience of Yahweh, the God of their fathers. Myth was no longer an effort to escape the death mercilessly embedded in every now of time. They historicized the ancient myths of creation, life and death by transforming them into the genesis of history. Creation provided the setting of history; the emergence of life its beginning; death its foil. They situated themselves in a universe which reflects its creator and in a history which expressed his personal revelation and concern for them. The Lord of creation reached out to man in the unfolding of history. Rather than a mythical escape from history, salvation was a meeting with God in man's own commitment to history.

The Bible saw man as called to fulfill an historical mission within the universe. God created man in his own image and after his own likeness. He gave him "dominion over the fish of the sea, the birds of the air, and the cattle, and over all the wild animals and all the creatures that crawl on the ground" (Gen. 1:26). He blessed him and made him fertile that he might multiply, fill the earth and subdue it (Gen. 1:28). Adam was God's co-creator. He too would beget sons in his own likeness and after his own image. Created by God, man would consciously bring himself into being by co-creating. In need of divine salvation, man would be saved by fulfilling his own salvific mission in history.

Our solidarity with biblical history calls for the same creative commitment to history on the part of us all. If we really want to pray with the Scriptures, we cannot pick and choose among the various aspects of biblical man's attitude toward history. We cannot remain passive, we must be active participants in a divine history which includes us.

Personal History

The special insight and historical vision which saw God's unifying presence in history was one of faith. The Israelite, the Jew and the early Christian knew God in the present moment, but not as an isolated moment. He related this experiential knowledge of God not only to past generations of religious history, but also to his own relatively brief personal history. God who had been present to him in the past, who had known him even before he was formed in his mother's womb (Jer. 1:5), continued to be present and to reveal himself now. This continuity in each individual's personal history enabled him to develop a healthy religious self-concept.

Some of the autobiographical passages in Paul's letters may be interpreted in this context. While these sections are pastorally directed to the reader and are usually exhortatory or apologetical in their intent, they do indicate the apostle's effort at synthesizing his personal history. The various functions and qualifications given by the apostle in the opening address of his letters actually summarize the different aspects of his historical self-concept. "Greetings from Paul, a servant of Christ Jesus, called to be an apostle and set apart to proclaim the gospel of God... favored with apostleship, that we may spread his name and bring to obedient faith all the Gentiles" (Rom. 1:1, 5). This view of himself had emerged through reflection on his many years of actual experience as a dedicated Jew and Christian.

Paul demonstrates the same historical sensitivity in the thanksgiving passages of his letters. Following the opening address, with the exception of the letter to the Galatians, Paul reviews and sums up the history of his addressees' involvement with the Gospel:

> I give thanks to my God every time I think of you — which is constantly, in every prayer I utter — rejoicing, as I plead on your behalf, at the way you have all continually helped promote the gospel from the very first day (Phil. 1:3-5).

In these passages Paul constantly alludes to his own prayer on behalf of his addressees. He also concludes with a prayer adapted to the history and present circumstances of the people for whom he is writing:

> My prayer is that your love may more and more abound, both in understanding and wealth of experience, so that with a clear conscience and blameless conduct you may learn to value the things that really matter, up to the very day of Christ. It is my wish that you may be found rich in the harvest of justice which Jesus Christ has ripened in you, to the glory and praise of God (Phil. 1:9-11).

In First Thessalonians, the thanksgiving passage takes up all of the first three chapters, aside from the initial one-verse greeting. This passage which recalls the origins and early history of the church in Thessalonica concludes with the following prayer:

> What thanks can we give to God for all the joy we feel in his presence because of you, as we ask him fervently night and day that we may see you face to face and remedy any shortcomings in your faith? May God himself, who is our Father and our Lord Jesus make our path to you a straight one! And may the Lord increase you and make you overflow with love for one another and for all, even as our love does for you. May he strengthen your hearts, making them blameless and holy before our God and Father at the coming of our Lord Jesus with all his holy ones (3:9-13).

Not only was Paul's prayer rooted in man's historical involvement in religious experience. History itself was such as to overflow into an expression of prayer. Paul's religious view of the historical past provided the grounds for trusting faith in the present and constituted the basis for hope in the future.

The Old and New Testament reflect a definite, if oftentimes implicit, attitude toward creation and history. God revealed himself to man through a history which gradually unfolded in the arena of creation. The Scriptures witness to biblical man's deep-rooted historical solidarity.

The Deuteronomist's prayer was founded on prior history. Kerygmatic prayer was based on an even longer period of history. Both the Israelite and the early Christian identified with that history. He extended the continuum of history into the present to include himself, his challenges and his commitments within it. Historical formulations of prayer came to life for him because he himself participated in the same history which had generated them.

If we wish to pray with the Scriptures, we too must share their historical consciousness. How can we expect an historically-based prayer to come to life for us, if we view ourselves outside of biblical or divine history? We do have a bridge from the biblical past to the present: historical solidarity. There is a path from our world to that of the Old and New Testaments. "My father was a wandering Aramean." Biblical prayer can be our personal prayer. "Christ died for our sins."

Community Consciousness

We, many though we are, are one body.
—1 Cor. 10:17

Maturity calls for an ability to relate socially as well as to situate oneself historically. In our effort to achieve personhood, in our struggle for self-actualization, we easily lose sight of our human community and turn in upon ourselves. Considerable effort toward personal growth is misdirected. Much energy is frustrated.

A person's relationships with his fellow man constitute an essential element of selfhood. We grow in personhood through our community relationships. Selfhood is achieved in the context of community. Separation from the community is self-destructive.

Prayer is the activity of one who actively reaches out of himself to others. It is the activity of a human being in community. Apart from a community attitude, prayer is impossible. We can well understand why one who finds community relationships difficult or who is struggling with his own identity is usually unable to pray. Prayer is incompatible with social alienation.

Prayer is the activity of a person. Once a minimal degree of personhood has been achieved, prayer becomes a potent source of personal growth. This minimal level of development is usually assured through the normal set of human relationships found in the intimacy of the family. The quality of adult prayer depends to a large extent on the manner in which the critical challenges of early childhood, adolescence and young adulthood have been met. Prayer is thus a good indicator of one's developmental adjustment.

We should not be surprised to discover that biblical literature is very much an expression of prayer. The community dimension of life was extremely pronounced among biblical peoples. The family effectively provided the basic unit of society. There were exceptions, but in general both young and old were secure in their belongingness. The village, the city, the tribal area and the nation all responded to various levels of man's social needs.

At each period of history, God's self-revelation took place within the community, and man responded precisely as a member of the community. Biblical man prayed in a community context. There was family prayer over which the father presided. There were times of prayer for the entire village or city. There were national religious celebrations and holydays when the whole of Israel affirmed its unity in a communal relationship to the living God.

At times, God revealed himself in a community experience, and man responded in a community prayer. At other times, God revealed himself to a single individual, but even here divine inspiration was directed to the community. It is as a member of the community that the individual opened himself to God and responded.

Biblical prayer can never become our prayer unless we too are men and women of community. The challenge is especially serious in view of the alienation of so many in contemporary society. "We are the hollow men!"

The Old Covenant

In the Old Testament, Israel's community solidarity was expressed in various ways. Israel was the flock, the royal people and the spouse of Yahweh. The most basic of all Old Testament themes, however, was that of the covenant, which underlies every other expression of Israelite unity.

Throughout its history, Israel viewed itself as the people with whom the God of the fathers, Yahweh, had formed a covenant. This special covenant was seen to stem from the time of Israel's constitution as a people at the foot of Mount Sinai. Prior to the experience of Sinai, the Mosaic covenant had been prepared by earlier covenants granted to Israel's ancestors. The Priestly Writers of the sixth and fifth centuries B.C. considered Hebrew and Israelite covenant history to be a renewal of the community-peace and belongingness of creation, when no covenant was needed, since man was already at peace with God, with himself and with his fellow man.

The notion of covenant was drawn ultimately from the Hittite people, a powerful nation based in central Turkey which flourished in the second millennium B.C. As one of the dominant powers in the Middle East, the Hittites developed a number of legal institutions to govern their political, economic and military relationships with other nations.

With major powers such as existed in Egypt and Mesopotamia, the Hittites established bilateral or parity treaties, in which both powers bound themselves by oath to reciprocal obligations. In the case of kingdoms and princedoms which they dominated, they imposed vassal or suzerainty treaties, in which the inferior power alone assumed various obligations under oath. The gods were invoked as witnesses to the treaty at its conclusion, and the text was deposited in a sacred place.

Early in Israel's history, the Hittite treaty institutions greatly influenced the manner in which the various Israelite tribes gathered together into a confederation. From its similarity with the Hellenic twelve-tribe confederations, this type of relatively loose Israelite unity about a central sanctuary has been termed an amphictyony. The Israelites, however, referred to it as a *berith* or covenant, an extremely ancient term with strong ritual and liturgical connotations. On the model of Hittite treaty institutions, God was invoked as a witness to Israel's ancient tribal covenant.

As Israel continued to reflect on its historical experience of unity as well as on its relationship to God, the nature of Israel's covenant unity underwent a radical transformation. The covenant became a powerful theological model to express Israel's relationship to God. No longer was God viewed simply as a witness to the covenant. He became an actual party to it. The Hittite vassal or suzerainty treaty, and not the parity treaty was used to formulate this new set of relationships. In no way was God the equal of his people. As sovereign Lord, he gratuitously offered Israel a covenant, and Israel bound itself to accept its terms. The clauses of the covenant were formulated in the decalogue.

As is clear from its most basic theological formulation, Yahweh's covenant was not totally void of reciprocity: "I will take you as my own people, and you shall have me as your God" (Exod. 6:7). The Lord promised to be present to his people and to guide them so long as they remained faithful to its clauses. Israel was the real beneficiary of the covenant, not God. A faithful Israel was assured of God's loving mercy *(hesed)* and constant fidelity *('emet)*,

> All the paths of the Lord are kindness (*hesed*) and
> constancy (*'emet)*
> toward those who keep his covenant and his
> decree (Ps. 25:10).

Israel would enjoy God's peace *(shalom)*,

> I will make with them a covenant of peace; it shall be an everlasting covenant with them, and I will multiply them, and put my sanctuary among them forever (Ez. 37:26).

The term covenant did not refer exclusively to Israel's union with God. It still included Israel's inter-tribal unity. The twelve tribes of Israel were united to one another in a covenant relationship with Yahweh. With the emergence of greater Israelite unity, the tribal organization of Israel diminished in importance. Accordingly, the covenant came to refer to the inter-personal unity binding each Israelite to his people. The Israelites were the people of the covenant, united to one another as brothers in a common divine covenant.

The synthesis of Israel's social unity within a divine covenant is well presented in Exod. 24:3-8, one of the classical texts concerning the establishment of the Sinaitic covenant. First, we see how God himself dictated the terms of the covenant through the person of its mediator Moses. The people of Israel responded with a communal statement of commitment. They were addressed as a community and they responded as one:

> When Moses came to the people and related all the words and ordinances of the Lord, they all answered with one voice, 'We will do everything that the Lord has told us'.

Both the words of the Lord and the people's commitment were then memorialized. The words were inscribed in the book of the covenant as a permanent record of the covenant which had been offered. The book of the covenant corresponded to the Hittite treaty documents, which were deposited in a sacred place for future reading on various occasions. Twelve pillars symbolized the twelve tribes of Israel. They would stand as a reminder to the Israelites of their commitment to the covenant they had accepted:

> Moses then wrote down all the words of the Lord and, arising early the next day, he erected at the foot of the mountain an altar and twelve pillars for the twelve tribes of Israel.

The Israelite covenant was established in a ritual context. Blood from sacrifices was splashed on the altar and sprinkled over the people. The use of blood was highly appropriate since for Israelites and other ancient Near Eastern peoples blood signified life itself. God and people were thus united in one life:

> Then, having sent certain young men of the Israelites to offer holocausts and sacrifice young bulls as peace offerings to the Lord, Moses took half of

> the blood and put it in large bowls; the other half he splashed on the altar. Taking the book of the covenant, he read it aloud to the people, who answered, 'All that the Lord has said, we will heed and do'. Then he took the blood and sprinkled it on the people, saying, 'This is the blood of the covenant which the Lord has made with you in accordance with all these words of his.'

The covenant thus represented a most basic set of relationships involving both God and the Israelite people. Union with God implied union with his people. Separation from God's people meant estrangement from God. Law was viewed as the ethical code of the covenant, governing both social relationships and religious attitudes. Worship celebrated the various aspects of the covenant relationship. Its sacrifices were aimed at achieving covenant reconciliation and assuring the blessing of peace. Its prayer was the response of a covenanted people to an ever faithful God.

We can understand how for Israel's religious historians, history was the story of Israel's covenant relationship with Yahweh, of the manner in which the Lord was faithful and true to his covenant even in the face of Israel's infidelity. The role of the prophets was to awaken Israel's sense of covenant commitment, to call Israel to fidelity. Wisdom writers taught the practical way of covenant living.

The New Covenant

Covenant terminology and theology can also be found in the New Testament. At a very early date, the Christians saw themselves as belonging to a new covenant in Christ's blood. As in the Old Testament, the context of the covenant was largely liturgical.

The Greek word *diatheke* which the Septuagint had utilized to translate *berith* into Greek appears especially in the old eucharistic formulae. In their breaking of the bread, the Christians were united to one another in a common union with God.

For the early Christians the sharing in the one life of God thus took on extraordinary realism. The blood of the covenant was the blood of its mediator, Jesus Christ. By sharing in the life of the Son of God, the Christians themselves grew in divine sonship.

Aside from the eucharistic formulae and the epistle to the Hebrews, explicit use of the word covenant is relatively rare in the New Testament. The notion and reality of the covenant, however, is all-pervasive as a very strong undercurrent. The Christians had been formed in the covenant. In the early years of Christianity, covenant theology continued to provide a matrix for developing the various theological dimensions of life. The kingdom with its royal people, the good shepherd with his faithful flock, the spouse with his bride, each of these New Testament images was actually a translation of covenant relationships into other metaphorical terms. We need not presuppose that such translations were done consciously. They had long been part of the very air Israel breathed.

The critical difference between the new and the old covenant was the person of Christ. The advent of the personal presence of God among his people transformed the set of relationships which obtained in the Old Testament. No longer was God merely a party to the covenant. God actually shared in the humanity of the covenant people. In Christ, God's law was truly inscribed in the heart of man. The old deuteronomic law of love became a new commandment.

In Christ, God penetrated the brotherhood of those who responded to his covenant. In Christ, man's response to God's covenant invitation truly reflected the divine initiative.

> In times past, God spoke in fragmentary and varied ways to our fathers through the prophets; in this, the final age, he has spoken to us through his Son, whom he has made heir of all things and through whom he first created the universe. This Son is the reflection of the Father's being, and he sustains all things by his powerful word (Heb. 1:1-3).

Our new and everlasting covenant is in Christ. By sharing in the life of him who is the head of the body, the church, and the first-born of the dead (Col. 1:18), our covenant response shares in that of Christ. It is transformed by the response of him who is the image of the invisible God and the first-born of all creatures (Col. 1:15).

The Christian community of divine life was sometimes referred to as a *koinonia.* The term implied brotherhood, fellowship, fraternal solidarity and common life. In the old covenant context, God's people had enjoyed *koinonia* among themselves. This *koinonia* was created by the people's relationship to God, but God himself was not included in the *koinonia.* With the advent of Christ, the Christians enjoyed *koinonia* with the Lord.

For Luke, *koinonia* was one of the distinguishing characteristics of the Christian community, along with the listening to the teaching of the apostles, the breaking of the bread and the prayers. For Paul, the eucharistic meal itself was the expression of the *koinonia*. The Eucharist both presupposed and strengthened the bonds of *koinonia*.

The Christian community was the body of Christ, his very members (1 Cor. 12:27). For Christians to be disunited was to tear asunder the body of Christ: "Has Christ, then, been divided into parts?" (1 Cor. 1:13). The Christians were born with Christ, they suffered with him and they died with him.

United to Christ, the Christians were united to one another in Christ. Not only did they share in Christ's suffering; they also shared in one another's suffering.

> I have already said that you are in our hearts, even to the sharing of death and life together (2 Cor. 7:3).
>
> If one member suffers, all the members suffer with it; if one member is honored, all the members share its joy (1 Cor. 12:26).

Covenant Prayer

In light of the basic covenant attitudes of both the Old and the New Testaments, we may appreciate the community consciousness of God's people at prayer. Biblical prayer requires that we find God present in our historical community. The biblical covenant is our covenant. Like the Israelites and Christians of long ago, we too must be sensitive to God's voice in community. Like them, we must respond to him in community solidarity.

Shall we pray with the Scriptures? Let us sing the praises of the God of our fathers. Let us thank him for the benefits of his covenant, especially for the continuing gift of life in his presence. Let us exult at the good news of a covenant which never grows old. Let us speak our repentance and seek forgiveness for failures in living up to our covenant commitment. Let us beg God for his continued blessing and for all the things we need as his covenanted people.

As a community prayer, our biblical prayer is very frequently expressed in the first person plural. *We, us, our,* these are the normal pronouns of biblical prayer.

> Come let *us* bow down in worship;
> let *us* kneel before the Lord who made *us.*
> For he is *our* God,
> and *we* are the people he shepherds, the flock he guides (Ps. 95:6-7).

Each member speaks the prayer of the entire community.

> Give *us* today *our* daily bread (Matthew 6:11).

When our prayer is expressed in the first person singular, it readily moves into the first person plural. The transition is hardly noticeable.

> *My* father was a wandering Aramean...
> When the Egyptians maltreated and oppressed *us*...
> *We* cried to the Lord (Deut. 26:5-7).

The *I* finds its full identity only in its relationship to the *we.* The *I, me, my* is the pronoun of many members of the community praying as one. Each one's personal *I* is the personification of the entire covenant people.

There are times when the *I* is more personal.

> Hearken to my words, O Lord,
> attend to my sighing.
> Heed my call for help,
> my king and my God! (Ps. 5:2-3).

Even here, the *I* addresses God in awareness of its responsibility to the community.

> But let all who take refuge in you
>   be glad and exult you forever.
> Protect them, that you may be the joy
>   of those who love your name.
> For you, O Lord, bless the just man;
>   you surround him with the shield of your good
>   will (Ps. 5:12-13).

Cut off from the community, deported from Jerusalem, how could we pray?

> By the streams of Babylon
>   we sat and wept
>   when we remembered Zion.
> On the aspens of that land
>   we hung our harps,
> Though there our captors asked for us
>   the lyrics of our songs,
>   and our despoilers urged us to be joyous!
>   'Sing for us the songs of Zion!'
> How could we sing a song of the Lord
>   in a foreign land? (Ps. 137:1-4).

Well might we sing at the toss of a coin or at the crack of a whip, the song of a slave. But we are not slaves. We are not performers. This would not be our song. It would not be a song of the Lord.

How often we have joined a sinful Adam, exiled from God's presence and condemned to death. How often we have wandered off to Babylon in voluntary exile. We were too good for the community of God's poor. Babylon was glamour, pleasure, power, fame and riches. Faithless spouses, prodigal sons, we threw away our heritage. Far from the community, we heard the sentence of covenant death. But the sentence was always conditional. The voice of a new Adam repeatedly called to us in our exile: "I am the resurrection and the life" (John 11:25). Freedom could yet be ours. Our place at the Christian table awaited us. "Praised be the God and Father of our Lord Jesus Christ" (Eph. 1:3).

> If I forget you, Jerusalem,
> may my right hand be forgotten!
> May my tongue cleave to my palate
> if I remember you not,
> If I place not Jerusalem
> ahead of my joy (Ps. 137:5-6).

Like the Israelite, the Christian is his brother's keeper. Like Christ, he is a man for others. His community consciousness includes a sense of responsibility for creating the community. All of biblical literature is ultimately directed at the ongoing formation of the covenant community. Such must be the attitude of anyone who would pray with the Scriptures.

Open to the Future

For his mercy endures forever.
—Ps. 136:1

Biblical prayer is a recapitulation of history. To express his faith in prayer, biblical man recalled the manner in which God had been present to him in the experience of his race and in his own personal experience. The present moment had religious meaning within the context of the historical continuum to which it belonged. Without such historical faith, prayer is apt to be a meaningless leap into the dark.

Biblical prayer is also an expression of community vitality. God's historical manifestations took place in the community. Prayer was one of biblical man's community responses. The quality of community prayer depended in large measure on the degree in which a number of people or a population had solidified its bonds of charity and achieved true community. The quality of personal prayer depended on the manner in which the individual identified with the community and shared in its life. Paraphrasing St. Paul, we might say that without love's community consciousness, biblical prayer is nothing.

There is yet a third dimension to the attitude of biblical prayer. God who manifested himself in the present and in ages past would continue to do so. Our biblical forbears looked to the future with hope. Here lay the ultimate touchstone of their prayer. Here lies our final challenge. To pray with the Bible, we must share its hopeful attitude of personal openness. Historical and social solidarity are not the only conditions for mature biblical prayer. Maturity in our life with God calls for unstinting openness to the future.

Future Directed

Biblical prayer was inherently future-directed. It refused to enclose itself within the discernible bounds of the past. It rejected any absolutizing of the present moment. Surely, the present was the end-point of a long historical continuum. But it was also a starting point, the beginning of future history. For the community this meant openness to ongoing life, to new and unforeseen situations, to new self-realizations and to constant renewal.

Psalm 136 is an excellent example of Israel's future-directedness at prayer. As a hymn of thanksgiving (vv. 1-3, 26), this psalm extols the Lord's goodness (v. 1) in both creation (vv. 4-9) and history (vv. 10-22). It surveys the great wonders of the earth's genesis, the heavens which the Lord made in wisdom, the earth which he spread out over the waters, the great lights with the sun to rule over the day and the moon and stars to rule over the night. It reviews the marvelous events of Israel's exodus from Egypt, from the smiting of the Egyptians in their first-born, to the troubled sojourn in the wilderness, and the granting of a land as a heritage to Israel his servant. God remembered Israel in its abjection and freed it from its foes (vv. 23-24).

Israel's gratitude does not stem purely from the things which God wrought in the past. Creation and history are recalled in light of God's continuing goodness: God is the one "who alone *does* great wonders" (v. 4) and "who *gives* food to all flesh" (v. 25). God's wonders and gifts are not limited to any moment of history. The full reason for Israel's gratitude is precisely that the Lord's "mercy endures forever." In remembrance of the past, Israel stands in the present and faces the future. As the soloist sang out each of the wonders of creation and history, the entire people repeatedly punctuated his recital with its profession of confidence and hope: "for his mercy endures forever."

Beneath the heavens, the earth will forever lie upon the waters. Forever will the great lights rule over day and night. The Lord will remember Israel in its abjection and free it from its foes. His wonders will never cease. His nourishment will never fail.

The book of Deuteronomy, with its emphasis on the *today* of the Sinaitic covenant, was also essentially future-directed.

> For this command which I enjoin on you today is not too mysterious and remote for you. It is not up in the sky, that you should say, 'Who will go up in the sky to get it for us and tell us of it, that we may carry it out?' Nor is it across the sea, that you should say, 'Who will cross the sea to get it for us and tell us of it, that we may carry it out?' No, it is something very near to you, already in your mouths and in your hearts; you have only to carry it out (Deut. 30:11-14).

At each moment of its future history, Israel would ever be able to respond to the covenant. God would always continue to extend his covenant invitation. The covenant would always be *today*.

In Paul's expression of gratitude to the Christians of Philippi, past and present accomplishment is but a prelude to prayer. The Philippians had "continually helped promote the gospel from the very first day" (1:5). They now shared Paul's gracious lot as he lay in prison or was summoned to defend the solid ground on which the gospel rests (1:7). In his prayer he confronted their future with hope.

> My prayer is that your love may more and more abound, both in understanding and wealth of experience, so that with a clear conscience and blameless conduct you may learn to value the things that really matter, up to the very day of Christ (1:9-10).

Paul's prayerful hope was not unfounded or without criteria. Hope was firmly grounded in historical experience.

> We know that affliction makes for endurance, and endurance for tested virtue, and tested virtue for hope (Rom. 5:3-4).

The objectiveness of this hope could be verified in the experience of God's love.

> And this hope will not leave us disappointed, because the love of God has been poured out in our hearts through the Holy Spirit who has been given to us (Rom. 5:5).

Expectations

Biblical prayer confronted the future with a set of expectations. History was interpreted as a number of promises first issued to Abraham. There were promises of continuing life through an undying posterity.

> I will make of you a great nation, and I will bless you (Gen. 12:2).
>
> Look up at the sky and count the stars, if you can. Just so shall your descendants be (Gen. 15:5).

There were promises of a land where Israel would forever flourish.

> To your descendants I will give this land (Gen. 12:7).
>
> . . . a good and spacious land, a land flowing with milk and honey (Exod. 3:8).

Israel expected those promises to be fulfilled in the face of every contradiction. Sarah was barren. God asked Abraham to offer his only son in holocaust. Israel found herself slaving at the construction of Pharaoh's cities in Egypt. The Assyrians despoiled the entire northern territory. Babylon destroyed Jerusalem and deported the pride of her citizenry to the banks of the Euphrates. In spite of all, Israel prayed. Ever expectant, forever threatened, Israel still managed to hope and to pray. Prayer was consciously directed at the continuing fulfillment of God's promises. When expectations failed to materialize, Israel turned to God with an anguished cry.

> O Lord, hear my prayer,
> and let my cry come to you.
> Hide not your face from me
> in the day of my distress.
> Incline your ear to me;
> in the day when I call, answer me speedily
> (Ps. 102:2-3).

Crushed by contradictory situations, Israel languished in seeming hopelessness.

> For my days vanish like smoke,
> and my bones burn like fire.
> Withered and dried up like grass is my heart;
> I forget to eat my bread.
> Because of my insistent sighing
> I am reduced to skin and bone.
> I am like a desert owl;
> I have become like an owl among the ruins
> (Ps. 102:4-7).

But in her distress, Israel prayed. God would yet respond. Jerusalem destroyed would be rebuilt.

> But you, O Lord, abide forever,
> and your name through all generations.
> You will arise and have mercy on Zion,
> for it is time to pity her,
> for the appointed time has come.
> For her stones are dear to your servants,
> and her dust moves them to pity (Ps. 102:13-15).

Future generations would sing the praises of a Lord who had heeded his people's prayer.

> Let this be written for the generations to come,
> and let his future creatures praise the Lord:
> 'The Lord looked down from his holy height,
> from heaven he beheld the earth,
> To hear the groaning of the prisoners,
> to release those doomed to die' —
> That the name of the Lord may be declared in Zion;
> and his praise, in Jerusalem,
> When the peoples gather together,
> and the kingdoms, to serve the Lord
> (Ps. 102:19-23).

In the New Testament, the apostle Paul agonized over the unexpected blindness of his fellow Jews. For Paul, Christ came in fulfillment of Israelite history. Without Christ, that history drifted rudderless in aimless darkness. Why did his fellow Jews, his teachers, his rabbinical colleagues, and his friends, why did his people not accept Christ? Surely God had predestined them to be his everlasting people! He had given them everything. But the facts were plain. Christ and his message was not being accepted into the mainstream of Jewish life. Why could they not see?

> I speak the truth in Christ: I do not lie. My conscience bears me witness in the Holy Spirit that

> there is great grief and constant pain in my heart. Indeed, I could even wish to be separated from Christ for the sake of my brothers, my kinsmen the Israelites. Theirs were the adoption, the glory, the covenants, the law-giving, the worship, and the promises; theirs were the patriarchs, and from them came the Messiah (I speak of his human origins) (Rom. 9:1-5).

It could not all have been in vain. Paul faced his frustrated expectations with a prayer.

> Blessed forever be God who is over all! Amen (Rom. 9:5).

Had God not been present to Paul in Christ, that would have been a blind prayer. Solid in historical faith, however, and sensitive in love, it was a challenge to renew his search for understanding. Paul pursues that search throughout chapters nine, ten and eleven of his letter to the Christians at Rome.

Search for Meaning

Paul responded to reality's challenge with a thorough re-reading of history. Somehow, all would work out, in a marvelous manner, however unforeseen.

> How deep are the riches and the wisdom and the knowledge of God! How inscrutable his judgments, how unsearchable his ways! For 'who has known the mind of the Lord? Or who has been his counselor? Who has given him anything so as to deserve return?' For from him and through him and for him all things are. To him be glory forever. Amen (Rom. 11:33-36).

Paul's continuous search for meaning, divine meaning, provides a paradigm for everyman's search for meaning. Just as did Paul, and so many others whose prayer is classically recorded in the Scriptures, our prayer must seek to discern the word of God as expressed through the events and circumstances of the life we have set out to live. Every new moment of history is enigmatic: "How inscrutable his judgments, how unsearchable his ways!"

We seek out life's meaning in light of the past, realizing that the future will never be a mathematical summation of historical factors. The future will always mark a new creation, whose meaning becomes clarified progressively, as gradually the future itself finds its place in history.

Each prayerful expression of hope represents a stage in the conscious formulation of God's self-revelation. For us, God's forever is past, present and future. The past stretches out behind us; the present slips through our efforts to grasp it; the future always lies ahead, always new, always vital, as the temporal disclosure of God's forever for man who is not forever. Prayer never ceases to be a search for God's self-manifestation, an open quest for the word. Each discovery is the beginning of a new search. The search is never-ending. That God will continue to be present, that we cannot doubt. How he will be present, there lies the uncertainty. That is what we must discover.

The entire Old and New Testament is the record of such a search. When we lose sight of the search, when we close off the future, even the past and present become garbled. They may have been revelatory at one time, but no longer. History, which had reflected God's loving concern, loses the meaning it once had. Without the future, God's forever dissolves into a nightmare of apocalyptic meaninglessness. We become pathetic figures of Job, struck down in our expectations, beating our heads in a wasted effort to maintain the recent present or to restore the past. We rail at our plight and curse the past for the moment we were born.

> Perish the day on which I was born,
> the night when they said, 'the child is a boy!'
> May that day be darkness:
> let not God above call for it,
> nor light shine upon it!
> May darkness and gloom claim it,
> clouds settle upon it,
> the blackness of night affright it!
> May obscurity seize that day;
> let it not occur among the days of the year,
> nor enter into the count of the months!
> (Job 3:3-6).

What role can we play in a meaningless future? Let the Fates govern our destiny. Let the palmist read the lines of our efforts and failures and mysterious encounters. Life's geography is clearly fixed in a universal atlas. Let the medium peer into the crystal of illness, suffering and death. Let the convergence of stellar and planetary phenomena govern the day's activity. Life's calendar is already determined by the light-years of space. Satan and a host of demons have penetrated the world of men. How could we be responsible for a future which is not ours? Perhaps if we escape! Activity. Activity. Drugs. Heavier on the drums! Turn up the music! Louder! Louder! Perhaps if we join with evil. Satanic cults. Blood. Death. Let the world end in its universal agony. It is in the stars. Did not the Bible say that the world would end in a cataclysmic holocaust?

There is no escape. The world has not ended. "The word of our God stands forever" (Is. 40:8).

There is no evading a God in ceaseless covenant pursuit.

I fled Him, down the nights and down the days;
I fled Him, down the arches of the years;
I fled Him, down the labyrinthine ways
of my own mind; and in the mist of tears
I hid from Him, and under running laughter.
Up vistaed hopes, I sped;
and shot, precipitated,
Adown Titanic glooms of chasmed fears,
From those strong Feet that followed, followed after.

But with unhurrying chase,
and unperturbed pace,
Deliberate speed, majestic instancy,
They beat — and a Voice beat
More instant than the Feet —
'All things betray thee, who betrayest Me.'

— *Francis Thompson*[1]

Open to the Future

The past and present will once again have meaning when we accept the risks of life's commitment and open ourselves to the future. For man in a universe bound by time, the future is the point of man's meeting with mystery. God's self-revelation in the past is ever joined to the possibilities of his self-revelation in the future. Past and present are truly manifestations of God's forever only when they maintain their orientation to the mystery of the future, to an ongoing revelation which is never complete, to the yet-to-be-revealed.

Biblical prayer does not expect the past to be repeated or the present to be maintained. It is open

[1] Francis Thompson, *The Hound of Heaven.* London, Burns Oates & Washbourne Ltd., p. 7.

to unforeseen possibilities of fulfillment. Even when a prayer is very specific and its petitions are clearly determined by prior experience, it confronts the future as something open and undetermined. At its deepest level, biblical prayer is a plea that God's will be done.

The future, however, is not altogether blind. Prayer would become a fatalistic exercise in futility, a meaningless and hopeless "hope" that reality will correspond to our expectations, however unswervingly determined by fate, a kind of "Please, Lord, let your will have been mine! I know that what will happen will happen, but please let my will be done." Underlying biblical prayer is the certitude that just as God has made himself known in history and continues to make himself known in present experience, he will continue to reveal himself. In its openness, biblical prayer presupposes that the future will be revelatory.

Even when specific hopes seemed frustrated, hope continued to confront each new situation in its newness. Apart from such an attitude, the voice of prayer would have been stilled. No, there was no denying the past, which clearly had value and meaning. But neither was there any denying of the future whose meaning had yet to be discovered. The well-balanced biblical attitude accepted the past precisely as an open-ended promise for the future. Man's search for God was an adventure, not the cyclic rites of man's effort to recapture the past, not the staged thrill of one who assists at a drama, but the suspense of a real life, of a partially written play, whose next act has always yet to be written.

Our tendency is to return to the old and secure expectations and to close our eyes to a future tinted with threat. The Old and the New Testaments interpreted this tendency as testing God.

> Next the devil took him to the holy city,
> set him on the parapet of the temple, and said,
> "If you are the Son of God, throw yourself down.
> Scripture has it:
>> 'He will bid his angels take care of you;
>> with their hands they will support you
>> that you may never stumble on a stone' "
>> (Matthew 4:5-6).

As a sign of God's fidelity, man demanded that God maintain the past. God, however, had promised to be true to his word, not to man's shallow understanding of it. Man's denial of the future was countered by Jesus.

> Scripture has it:
>> 'You shall not put the Lord your God
>> to the test' (Matthew 4:7; Deut. 6:16).

By limiting the possibilities of the future we would destroy its mystery and blind ourselves to ongoing revelation. In an effort to reduce God to something definable, predictable and controllable, we would close off the possibilities of human life and history along with the many ways in which God can yet manifest himself through them. We would turn away from the mystery of our relationship with God. Our prayer must be rather that of Jesus:

> Abba (O Father), you have the power to do all things.
> Take this cup away from me.
> But let it be as you would have it,
> not as I (Mark 14:36).

Conclusion

No, the Bible is not dead. Like its prayer-book, the Psalter, "it is a living being who speaks, who suffers, groans and dies, who rises again and speaks on the threshold of eternity; who seizes one, bears one away, oneself and all the ages of time, from the beginning to the end" (A. Chouraqi).[1] Jeremiah did not deceive us. The Bible lives in our hearts, a prismed reflection of an ancient people's faith, a mirror image of everyman's search for God, a classical account of our own prayerful life with God.

True, we do not know how to pray as we ought, but the Spirit helps us in our weakness (Rom. 8:26). We have been reborn of an incorruptible seed and regenerated through the ever-living word of God (1 Peter 1:23). Respectfully, we turn the pages, and trace the story of our faith in biblical steps from the "Let-there-be-light" of Genesis to the "Come-Lord-Jesus" of Revelation. Sons of God, led by the Spirit of God, with each biblical word we cry "Abba!"

We have heard the call to prayer, a blast sounded by the Sons of Aaron on their trumpets of beaten metal (Sir. 50:16), tempered in the crucible of history. Nothing can excite like the word of God. The Bible lies open before us, two thousand years of religious tradition and literature, an unparalleled record of a

[1] A. Chouraqi, as quoted in *The Psalms*. New York, Paulist Press, 1968, p. 8.

people's experience of God, the word of God addressed to man in man's own words.

In the Old Testament we peer into the dim recesses of the mid-nineteenth century B.C. to find Abraham venturing forth from Haran in response to a call which profoundly marked the course of history. We stand in awe among the peaks and plains of the Sinai to join Moses, Israel's lawgiver, prophetic figure, and religious mediator, as he transforms a populous desert mass into a committed covenant people. We share in the prayer of David, Israel's military genius turned royal poet, and recall the heroic days when he created the nation and established its capital at Jerusalem. With the religious historian, we grow in self-understanding. At the voice of the prophet, we renew our covenant fidelity. In the school of the sage, we learn to live in the way of the Lord. Inspired by the Psalmist, we speak to God in song.

In the New Testament, we enter the religious chaos and conflict of the first century A.D. to find a clear-sighted Jesus announcing the coming of God's kingdom. In joyful expectation we join the company of Jesus and his disciples in their ascent to Jerusalem. The road to glory leads to Calvary hill: darkness, sorrow, fear, despair. Hope lies buried in a criminal's grave. Dawn breaks with a whisper: "The tomb is open. The tomb is empty." The whisper becomes a cry: "The Lord is risen! He has appeared to Simon!" In temple-court and market-place, Peter proclaims Jesus as Christ and Lord, the Son of God, risen to new life in the community of his followers. We follow in the path of Paul as he sets the Mediterranean world ablaze with the good news of One who was born of the stock of David according to the flesh, but who was made Son of God in power according to the spirit of holiness. With Mark, Matthew, Luke and John we grow in our personal knowledge of One who would mark the course of history even more profoundly than the awesome faith of Abraham.

No, the Bible is not dead. It lives in the hope of one who is committed to the future, in the charity of his community consciousness and in the faith of his historical solidarity. It lives in the today of one who lives life and who lives it with God. It lives in the spirit of one who has disciplined himself to serious study of both past and present, in the humility of one who acknowledges his ignorance. It lives in the response of one who is sensitive to a long biblical tradition of praying with the Scriptures, in the creativity of one who gives the Bible new life. From the heights of western history's massive *tell,* we have reached Jerusalem.

The tomb is open. The muted sounds have become a word, God's word, our word. We pray on the hillsides and by the sea, in brilliant sunlight and in the quiet of night. We pray at work and at play, in the theatre and in the classroom.

We pray in the breaking of the bread. Our Christian meal is an act of receiving, of adult receiving fulfilled in self-giving, in the sharing of our persons with those who have joined us at table. We open ourselves to our brother in Christ. Addressed to God, Christian prayer is a reaching out to our fellow man in Christian solidarity.

We pray in the peace of our chapels, quietly, reflexively, interiorizing the gift we have received, little by little overcoming the alienations of our civilization, becoming what we are, sons of God, created in the image and likeness of God.

There was a time when

> The Sons of Aaron would sound a blast,
> the priests, on their trumpets of beaten metal;
> A blast to resound mightily
> as a reminder before the Most High.
>
> Then all the people with one accord
> would quickly fall prostrate to the ground
> In adoration before the Most High,
> before the Holy One of Israel.
>
> Then hymns would re-echo,
> and over the throng sweet strains of praise
> resound.
> All the people of the land would shout for joy,
> praying to the Merciful One (Sirach 50:16-18).

The time is now.